Dear Michael,

Always keep your heritage in mind as you go forth in life.

Merry Christmas 2001.

Love,
Dad

THE BOOK OF
SCOTTISH CLANS

THE BOOK OF
SCOTTISH CLANS

IAIN ZACZEK

ILLUSTRATED BY JACQUI MAIR

BARNES
&NOBLE
B O O K S
NEW YORK

This edition published by Barnes & Noble, Inc., by arrangement with Cico Books Ltd

2001 Barnes & Noble Books

M 10 9 8 7 6 5 4 3 2 1

ISBN 0-7607-2590-X

First published in Great Britain in 2001 by Cico Books Ltd

32 Great Sutton Street London EC1V 0NB

Designed by David Fordham

Illustrations by Jacqui Mair

Typeset by MATS, Southend-on-Sea, Essex

Printed and bound in Portugal by Printer Portuguesa

Contents

INTRODUCTION

Scotland's clan system is unique, reflecting the richness and variety of the nation's cultural make-up, as well as the turbulence of its history. At heart, it is a tribal system, typical of all the Celtic peoples, but one which was modified over the centuries, to accommodate the arrival of invaders from the north and the south.

The nucleus of the Scottish nation was formed in 843, when the Picts and the Scots united under the leadership of Kenneth MacAlpin. Both groups were Celts and, as such, had already organized themselves along tribal lines. This worked like an extended family (*clann* is Gaelic for "children"), in which the chief served as the patriarchal figure. He was responsible for protecting the clan from its enemies, for settling disputes and for leading it on the battlefield. In return, he exercised complete authority over all its actions.

Within the clan, the ties of kinship were strengthened by other factors. Fostering was common, even when the parents of the children were still alive. The rearing of offspring by favored clan members was an honor, which created bonds that were as strong as blood-ties. In addition, there was manrent (payment for protection) and handfasting, a probationary form of marriage, which could end by mutual consent, if the couple failed to produce children. The clan could also offer protection to some groups who were not part of their immediate kin.

This included smaller clans, known as septs, or individual "broken" men, who were not linked to any particular clan.

Family members paid particular homage to their founding father, and his name was often preserved in the name of the clan. In most cases, the chosen ancestor was a distinguished, historical figure, although it might sometimes be a mythical hero. This harked back to earlier tribal times, when the clan would claim descent from a deity. Many of the newcomers, who settled in Scotland, adapted quite easily to this patronymic system. The MacLeods, for example, were descended from a Viking ancestor.

The main development of the clan system came with the introduction of feudalism. Hitherto, all land had been held in common by the tribe, but in a feudal society the king was responsible for its distribution. The greatest period of change occurred in the 12th century, when David I arrived to claim his throne. He was raised in England and, upon his succession, many of his Anglo-Norman retainers followed him to Scotland, where he gave them land. From this time on, many clans took their names from their estates.

THE CLANS

THE STORY OF THE GREAT CLANS forms the backbone of Scottish history. The Bruces and Stewarts founded royal dynasties, while others, such as the MacDonalds, the Douglases and the Campbells, created huge power blocs, which were effectively miniature kingdoms. Lower down the pecking order, clans were often awarded hereditary posts, to bind them to their mighty neighbors. These ranged from the Constable or Keeper of a strategic castle, to more mundane roles, such as physicians or armor-bearers.

The strength of these ties, which passed from generation to generation, could sometimes present problems. Clansmen were fiercely possessive about their traditional rights and domains, resisting any change that might be forced on them by a distant king. Feuding was endemic, and even something as minor as the clan's position within a battle formation could provoke bitter disputes. Periodic attempts were made to curb the lawlessness that could ensue from these quarrels although, from the point of view of the English authorities, it was the unwavering loyalty of the clans that posed the greatest threat. It is no accident that, after the Battle of Culloden (1746), the Government came to the conclusion that the only effective way to solve the Jacobite problem was to dismantle the entire clan system. Although officially abolished, ancient loyalties remain to this day.

Angus

Angus WAS AN extremely popular forename, with many variant spellings (Oenghus, Aeneas, Hungus), and this has led to much confusion about the clan's ancestor. The most distinguished contender is a 6th-century ruler named Oenghus, who was one of the co-founders of The Ancient Kingdom of Dalriada. There are close links with the McInnes clan, whose name means "Son of Angus."

Neil Armstrong carried a sample of his tartan with him during his moon walk

Armstrong

THE ORIGINS OF THE NAME of this famous Border clan appear to be surprisingly literal, for it was the nickname of their ancestor, who was known for his physical strength. The clan was granted lands in Liddesdale, where they acquired a fearsome, warlike reputation. In modern times, the astronaut Neil Armstrong carried a sample of his tartan with him during his moon walk.

BALFOUR

THIS IS A TERRITORIAL NAME, deriving from the Barony of Balfour at Markinch, in Fife. The first recorded use of the name came in 1304, when John de Balfure was included on an assize list. The most notable family member was the British statesman, James Balfour (1848–1930), who was created Earl Balfour of Whittinghame.

BARCLAY

THE BARCLAYS CAME from Norman stock. Roger de Berchelai ("Beautiful Field") and his son crossed the Channel at the Conquest, continuing north in the retinue of the future Queen Margaret (1067). There, they were granted the lands of Towie. The latter, together with Urie and Mather, formed the three main branches of the family.

BAXTER

THIS NAME EVOLVED FROM *bakester*, an archaic term for a female baker. As an occupational family name, Baxter is found in many parts of Scotland, although it is particularly popular in Fife, Angus and Forfar. In the early 13th century, Reginald Baxtar witnessed a document at Wemyss in Fife, while Geffrei le Baxtere took an oath at Lossithe in Forfar (1296). In the following century, William Baxtare was listed as a crossbowman at Edinburgh Castle (1312), while Robert Baxter was a town councillor at Aberdeen (1398). The Baxters are traditionally regarded as dependents of the Macmillan clan.

The Brodie family came into prominence in the 17th century

BRODIE

THE FAMILY HAILS FROM Morayshire, where they held the barony of Brothie. This was confirmed in 1311, in a charter from Robert the Bruce. Little is known about the early history of the clan, since most of the relevant documents were lost in 1645, when Brodie Castle was fired by Lord Lewis Gordon. The family appears to have come to prominence in the 17th century, when Alexander Brodie of Brodie (1617–80) became one of the leading Covenanters. The most notorious member of the dynasty, however, was Deacon William Brodie, who led a double life as a respectable town councilor and a daring burglar. He was eventually hanged in 1788, on a set of gallows which he had designed himself and sold to the council.

BOWES-LYON

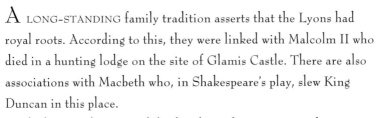

A LONG-STANDING family tradition asserts that the Lyons had royal roots. According to this, they were linked with Malcolm II who died in a hunting lodge on the site of Glamis Castle. There are also associations with Macbeth who, in Shakespeare's play, slew King Duncan in this place.

The historical origins of the family are less certain, perhaps emanating from Normandy and England. The name of Lyon is first recorded in Scotland in the 14th century, when Thomas Lyon was a crossbowman, serving in Edward II's garrison at Linlithgow (1311). A few decades later, John Lyon received a charter from David II, confirming his right to lands at Forteviot and Forgundenny in Perthshire (1342). A similar document, dating from 1372, recorded that John Lyon was appointed Thane of Glamis, and that his lands were erected into a free barony. His fortunes were enhanced still further when he married one of the daughters of Robert II (1376) and was made a royal chamberlain, though he came to a sorry end, being murdered in his bed in 1382.

Patrick Lyon was granted a peerage in 1445, but his descendants were temporarily deprived of their ancestral home when the widow of the 6th Lord of Glamis was accused of being a witch. The castle was soon returned, however, and the family went on to acquire the titles of Earl of Kinghorne (1606) and Earl of Strathmore.

"Bowes" was incorporated into the family name, following the 9th Earl's marriage to a wealthy English heiress, Mary Eleanor Bowes (1767). It was in 1923, however, that another marriage brought the family lasting fame. For on this occasion, Lady Elizabeth Bowes-

The ghost of a pageboy haunts Glamis Castle

Lyon, the youngest daughter of the 14th Earl, married the second son of George V. Following the abdication of his older brother, Edward VIII, he ascended the throne as George VI in 1936.

THE LEGEND OF BOWES-LYON

GLAMIS CASTLE is often reckoned to be one of the most haunted homes in the whole of Scotland. While the spectre of a colored page boy has been seen for centuries outside guest bedrooms, many legends revolve around a secret room, home to a supernatural inhabitant. As proof of this, it is said that if visitors to the castle count its windows, they will always find one more on the exterior building than on the inside of the castle. The most popular of the many tales about this secret room is that its occupant was the so-called "Beast of Glamis." According to tradition, this hideously deformed creature – which has been variously described as a huge, misshapen toad or a one-eyed cyclops – was the rightful earl. He was born in the 18th century, but the family were so ashamed of his shocking appearance that they constructed a concealed room for him, so that they could keep his existence a secret. The terrible truth was revealed to each new heir to the title as they came of age. In spite of his deformities, the "beast" was incredibly strong and lived for more than 200 years, before dying in the 1920s.

According to another legend, the hidden room contains a group of enchanted gamblers. At their head is Alexander, Earl of Crawford, a wicked laird who was nicknamed "Earl Beardie." He was playing cards with his cronies and losing so heavily that one of his companions suggested he should stop. At this, the earl went into a terrible rage and swore by the devil that he would play on until the Day of Judgement. No sooner had these words left his lips than the Horned One appeared at the table and joined their game. He will remain there, gambling with the wicked earl, until the last Trump is sounded.

Aristocratic gamblers are said to play eternal card games in the castle's secret chamber

BRUCE

THIS IS A TERRITORIAL NAME, deriving from the Norman castle of Brix or Brus, which was situated near Cherbourg. It was built in the 11th century by Adam de Brus, and a relative named Robert accompanied William I on the Conquest (1066). His son, also called Robert, followed David I to Scotland, when he went to claim his crown (1124), and was granted lands in Annandale.

The Bruces' ascent to the throne was launched in the 13th century, when the 4th Lord of Annandale married Isabella of Huntingdon, a niece of William the Lion (1142–1214), King of the Scots. This gave the family a viable claim to power, when the royal House of Dunkeld became extinct in 1290. Robert Bruce was one of thirteen contenders for this honor and, although on this occasion the successful candidate was John Balliol, his grandson – the celebrated Robert the Bruce – did eventually manage to secure the throne. He was crowned at Scone in 1306 and cemented his position with a famous victory at Bannockburn (1314), although the English did not formally recognize the situation until 1328.

The royal House of Bruce was comparatively short lived, ending with the death of David II (1371), but the clan had many other branches. From Sir Edward Bruce of Easter Kennet came the Bruces of Kinloss. He was granted the benefice of Kinloss Abbey in 1597, gaining the title of Lord Kinloss four years later. Later in the century, his descendants became the Earls of Elgin (1633) and Kincardine (1647). Thomas Bruce, 7th Earl of Elgin (1766–1841) courted controversy by bringing the Elgin Marbles from Athens in 1801 to London. Other branches include the Bruces of Airth, Clackmannan, Stenhouse and Balcaskie.

THE LEGEND OF BRUCE

Courage and brute determination were the qualities which won the crown for Robert the Bruce, enabling him to set his country on the road to independence. At times, however, some critics felt that he pushed his ambitions too far, ruthlessly disposing of anyone who blocked his path. This, at least, is the interpretation which some have placed on the confrontation with his rival, John Comyn, at the start of his career.

The fatal meeting was held at the Greyfriars' church in Dumfries in 1306, just a few months after Wallace's execution. With his death, Bruce and Comyn (Balliol's nephew) were now the obvious contenders for the leadership of the resistance movement, pitted against Edward I. The two men may have been hoping to resolve their differences but, whatever their intentions, a fight broke out and Comyn was killed.

The name Bruce derives from the Norman castle of Brus

Courage and brute determination won the crown for Robert the Bruce

Bruce's enemies claimed that he had murdered Comyn in cold blood and, in due course, he was excommunicated for killing a man on holy ground. For his part, Bruce hastened to Scone where, with dubious legality, he had himself proclaimed king. The Stone of Destiny had already been removed by the English, so he was obliged to use a makeshift throne and, in the absence of a genuine crown, a plain gold circlet was placed on his brow.

Edward had ample pretext for sending his forces to hunt down the rebel and, following two crushing defeats, Robert was forced into hiding. There is no historical record of his movements over the next few months, and it is to this bleak period that the celebrated fable of the spider is ascribed. According to the tale, the fugitive king was taking refuge in a cave. He was sick and disillusioned, convinced that the struggle for independence had failed. Then, as he languished in despair, he noticed a tiny spider swinging back and forth across the mouth of the cave, trying to anchor its web to the far side. Six times it failed, but on the seventh try it managed to achieve its goal. Bruce was encouraged by this show of determination, believing that it was meant as an object lesson for him. From that time on, he renewed his campaign against the English with added vigor, never looking back until he had achieved his victory at Bannockburn (1314).

In 1328, Robert was eventually reconciled with the Papacy and the excommunication was lifted. In gratitude, the king made it known, on his deathbed, that he wanted his heart to be carried on crusade. This task was entrusted to his faithful companion, Sir James Douglas. Accordingly, the heart was placed in a silver casket, which Douglas hung on a chain around his neck and took to Spain, where the Castilians were fighting a holy war against the Moors. During the battle, the Scottish forces became isolated from their allies and were about to be overrun. At this point, Douglas hurled the casket at the enemy, shouting: "Go first into the fray, brave heart, as you always did when you were alive." According to this version of events, the heart was eventually recovered and returned to Scotland, where it was buried in Melrose Abbey.

BURNS

T HIS IS A TERRITORIAL NAME, which probably stems from the Old English *burna* ("a brook"). The clan is traditionally associated with the Campbells, although the place name was so common that the family name can be found in most parts of Scotland. Robert Burns (1759–96, born Burness) is the Scottish nation's most famous poet.

CAMERON

T HE CAMERONS TAKE THEIR NAME from a Gaelic word, meaning "crooked nose" or "crooked hill." Initially, the clan was organized as a confederation of three influential families, the MacSorleys of Glen Nevis, the MacGillonies of Strone and the MacMartins of Letterfinlay. Subsequently, it divided into two main branches, the Camerons of Erracht and the Camerons of Lochiel. The most notable member of the latter was the Royalist, Sir Ewen Cameron of Lochiel, who was the last of the Highland chiefs to hold out against Cromwell during the Civil War (1642–9). His grandson Donald, better known as "Gentle Lochiel", also sided with the losing cause, when he joined Bonnie Prince Charlie in the 1745 uprising.

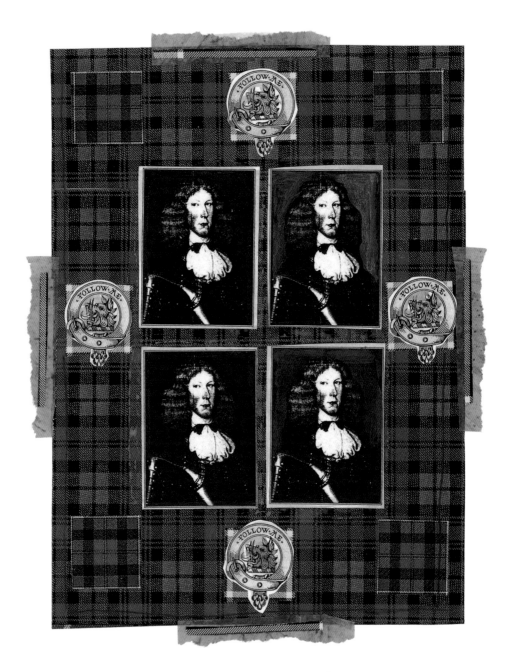

The Campbells were often known as the "Clan Diarmaid"

CAMPBELL

THIS CLAN NAME evolved from a personal epithet, for *cam-beul* is a
Gaelic term for "crooked mouth." This may have helped to promote
the family's association with another facial feature, for there is an old
tradition that the Campbells were descended from Diarmaid Ua
Duibne ("Diarmaid of the Love Spot"). As a result, they were often
known as the "Clan Diarmaid."

The clan can trace its roots back to the 13th century, when a certain
Gillespie Campbell was cited in a charter. By 1300, the family had
achieved greater prominence, for Colin Campbell of Lochawe was
knighted in 1280 and recognized as one of the most powerful lords in
the region. He was hailed as the founder of the Campbells of Argyll, and
subsequent chiefs were dubbed *MacCailean Mor* ("Son of Great Colin"),
as a reference to his Gaelic nickname. Sir Neil Campbell, Colin's son, was
granted extensive lands in the west Highlands, where the clan co-operated
with the crown in seeking to curb the power of the MacDonalds.

The Campbells of Breadalbane were as powerful as their Argyllshire
kinsmen. They were the descendants of Black Colin of Glenorchy, son
of Duncan Campbell of Lochawe. Their most influential family member
was Sir John Campbell who gave sterling support to Charles II and was
made Earl of Breadalbane (1681).

The most infamous moment in the clan's history occurred in 1692,
when a detachment of troops from the Campbells of Glenlyon took
part in the Massacre of Glencoe. During this nocturnal ambush, 38
MacDonalds were killed in their beds – an atrocity that drew
widespread condemnation, although the Campbells might argue that it
formed part of a long-running feud between the two clans.

THE LEGEND OF CAMPBELL

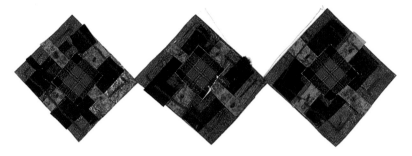

THE MASSACRE OF GLENCOE has been marked down in the annals as one of the darkest episodes in Scottish history. On the night of 13th February 1692, a detachment of Government troops, led by Robert Campbell of Glenlyon, launched a surprise attack on sleeping MacDonald clansmen. Some were killed in their beds, while others tried desperately to escape into the snow-capped hills. News of the slaughter provoked widespread condemnation, particularly since many of the soldiers had been billeted with the MacDonalds and had coexisted peacefully with them throughout the previous week. To most Scots, this breached the most fundamental laws of hospitality and it was for this reason, more than any other, that the event caused such an outcry. Blame fell upon the Campbells, in particular, partly because of their close links with the English government, and partly because of suspicions that John Campbell, 1st Earl of Breadalbane (1635–1717), had exploited the situation, in order to settle old scores with the MacDonalds.

The background to the massacre lay in the unstable political climate. In 1688, James VIII, the last of the Stuart kings, was driven out of power. William III, a Dutch Protestant, took his place on the English and Scottish thrones. James, meanwhile, set up a court in exile at Paris and plotted to regain his crown. As part of his plan, he landed in Ireland with an army, but was emphatically defeated at the Battle of the Boyne (1690). William proceeded to subdue his Irish domains, but was fully aware that Jacobite sympathies were still very strong in the Highlands of Scotland. So in an attempt to pacify the region, he ordered the clan chiefs to swear an oath of allegiance in return for financial rewards. The deadline for this oath was January 1 1692. Alasdair, 12th MacIain, the leader of the MacDonalds of Glencoe, agreed to sign the treaty on behalf of his clan. Through a fatal oversight, however, he traveled to Fort William rather than Inveraray, in order to make his submission. As a result, he was five days late in taking the oath. This offered the king's ministers a pretext for making an example of the recalcitrant Highlanders.

Most of the legends surrounding Glencoe have arisen after the night of the massacre. For, in spite of the element of surprise, comparatively few people were killed (just 38, less than a tenth of the number that had been targeted), and many of the most prominent clansmen managed to slip through the net. The most fanciful tale suggests that a band of fairy pipers swept through the glen, leading the attackers astray with their ghostly music. More realistically, there are stories that the Campbell soldiers helped their victims to escape. The most popular anecdote, which was repeated with endless variations, told of a warrior coming across a mother and child, huddling in the snow. Unable to bring himself to kill them, the soldier slew a dog or a wolf instead and took back his bloodied sword to show his commander, as evidence that he had carried out his cruel duty.

One other aspect of the massacre has entered Scottish folklore. Many Highlanders placed the ultimate blame for the killings on John Dalrymple, the Master of Stair (1648–1707) who, as William III's Secretary of State, gave the orders for the slaughter. Amid the ensuing recriminations, many critics focused on his coat of arms, which featured nine lozenges. Its similarity to the *Nine of Diamonds* soon prompted a superstition that the card was unlucky and, ever since then, it has been known colloquially as "the Curse of Scotland."

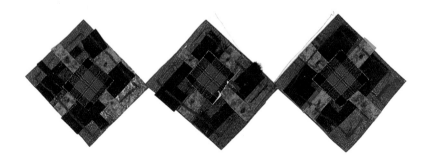

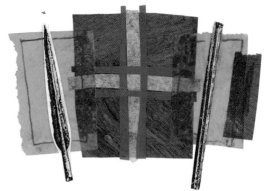

CARMICHAEL

THE FAMILY TAKES ITS NAME from the barony in upper Lanarkshire, which has been their ancestral home since the 13th century. The land belonged originally to the Douglases, but Sir John de Carmychell acquired it from William, Earl of Douglas, in 1374. Many of his descendants found fame in France, rather than Scotland. Sir John de Carmichael distinguished himself at the Battle of Beauge (1421), fighting for the French against the English. Another John Carmichael became Bishop of Orleans, instituting a Scottish mass (1429) for his fellow countrymen and officiating at the coronation of Charles VII. In France, he was known as Jean de St. Michel.

CARNEGIE

THE FAMILY TAKES ITS NAME from the lands of Carnegie in Angus. John de Ballinhard, who acquired these estates in 1358, is traditionally accepted as the founder of the Carnegies of Southesk. They were made Earls in 1633. Andrew Carnegie (1835–1918) was a successful steel magnate in the US, who made generous donations to his native land.

CHATTAN

UNLIKE MOST SCOTTISH CLANS, this name does not represent the fortunes of a single family. Instead, it refers to a confederation of various different clans, who grouped together for mutual protection.

St Cathan was one of the followers of St Columba

These include the Macphersons, the Macphails, the Mackintoshes, the Davidsons, the Shaws and the Farquharsons. The origins of the clan are disputed, but the popular view is that they were descended from Gille Chattan Mor ("Great Servant of Cathan"), a 13th-century chieftain. His name is a reference to St. Cathan, one of the followers of St. Columba. The sheer size of the Clan Chattan made it powerful, though there were frequent arguments over who should be its Captain (Chief).

COCKBURN

THIS CLAN TOOK ITS NAME from "Cukoueburn", a river in the Borders. Its use as a family name can be traced back to the end of the 12th century, when Peter de Cokburne was cited in a hospital charter.

Admiral Cockburn
took Napoleon
to St Helena

After this, the Cockburns became vassals of the Earl of March, eventually acquiring the Barony of Carriden. Subsequent clan members have distinguished themselves in very different fields: John Cockburn of Ormiston (1679–1758) was a pioneering agriculturalist; Henry Cockburn (1779–1854) was a Whig politician, a prominent judge and a campaigning pamphleteer; while Admiral Cockburn was charged with the task of conducting Napoleon Bonaparte to his place of exile on St. Helena (1815).

COLQUHOUN

THIS IS A TERRITORIAL NAME, stemming from an estate near Loch Lomond. Umphredus de Kilpatrick was the founder of the clan, acquiring the lands from the Earl of Lennox in the early 13th century. The chiefs later became hereditary keepers of Dumbarton Castle, and gained possession of the Barony of Luss through marriage (c.1368).

CRAWFORD

THE CLAN TOOK ITS NAME from their ancestral estates in Lanarkshire. The family was probably of Norman origin, arriving in Britain at the time of the Conquest, and there are 12th-century references to a Breton duke called Galfride de Crawford. The historical picture becomes clearer in the 13th century, when the death

The Crawford clan took its name from the ancestral estates in Lanarkshire

of Sir John Crawford was noted (1248), and when Sir Reginald Crawford was appointed Sheriff of Ayr (1296). The latter can be linked with the two main branches of the clan, the Crawfords of Auchinames and the Crawfords of Craufurdland. Margaret Crawford is well remembered as the mother of William Wallace.

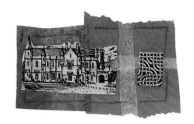

Cunningham

The name derives from the Cunningham district of Ayrshire, where the clan had settled by the mid-12th century. The name itself appears to be a combination of *cuinneag* ("milk pail") and *ham* ("village"). Hervey de Cunningham was granted land at Kilmaurs, after lending support to Alexander III, and the chiefs were later created Earls of Glencairn (1488).

Dalziel

The Dalziels took their name from their ancestral lands in Lanarkshire. The literal meaning of the word has been disputed, although it probably comes from the Gaelic *Dailghil* ("at the White Dale"). The clan chiefs became Earls of Carnwath (1649), and the best-known family member was General Thomas Dalyell (1599–1685), the "Muscovy Beast who roasted men."

Davidson

This is one of the many clans who sheltered under the banner of the Clan Chattan confederation. Previously, the family had been a sept of the Comyns, before changing allegiance in the 14th century.

*The Davidsons
rapidly moved
towards Inverness
and Aberdeen*

Their family name stems from David Dubh of Invernahaven, who was linked with the Mackintoshes. The Davidsons suffered from the internal divisions within Clan Chattan, which culminated in the bloody Battle of North Inch (1396). This strife may have prompted some clansmen to move to the northeast of Scotland, for the Davidsons rapidly gravitated towards Inverness and Aberdeen. The principal branches in the north were those of Cantray and Tulloch.

DEWAR

THE DEWARS ARE generally regarded as a sept of either the Menzies or the Macnabs. The name refers to the title of an important official, who was responsible for safeguarding any relics in the clan's possession. In the 14th century, for example, Donald Dewar Cogerach was the custodian of a crozier (*cogerach*), which had belonged to St. Fillan, an ancestor of the Macnabs. The name has become linked with a world-famous brand of whisky, as well as a type of vacuum flask, invented by Sir James Dewar (1842–1923). In recent times, it has also been associated with Donald Dewar (d. 2000), the First Minister of Scotland's new Parliament.

Douglas

THE NAME OF THIS FAMOUS CLAN has territorial origins. Douglas stems from the Gaelic *Dubh Glas* ("Dark Water"), which was a stream on one of their properties. In genealogical terms, however, the family's roots are surprisingly obscure. The name can be traced back only to the last quarter of the 12th century, when William de Douglas witnessed a charter for the monks of Kelso Abbey.

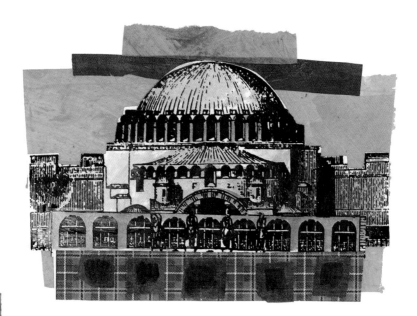

The first clansman of real prominence was Sir James Douglas (c.1286–1330). He figured prominently in the struggle for independence, capturing Roxburgh Castle (1314) and Berwick (1318). For his many services, Robert the Bruce rewarded him with property in Jedburgh, Galloway, and Lauderdale, together with an "Emerald Charter", which gave him exceptional powers within his own domain.

Sir James is hailed as the founder of the Black Douglases, who flourished as the leading branch of the clan until the 15th century. James's nephew, William, was made Earl of Douglas in c.1357, and the family fortunes were consolidated by Archibald "the Grim," the 3rd Earl. His successor campaigned successfully against the English in France, winning the Duchy of Touraine, but the clan was making dangerous enemies at home. This reached a climax in the 15th century, when the 8th Earl was killed by James II (1452), and the 9th Earl allied himself with the English, forfeiting his earldom in the process (1455).

After this, the chiefship passed to the Red Douglases, the Earls of Angus. Their most notable family member was Archibald, the 5th Earl, popularly known as "Bell-the-Cat." He earned this nickname by curbing royal power. Among other things, he slew the favourites of James III and abandoned James IV at Flodden (1513), following an argument on the battlefield.

THE LEGEND OF DOUGLAS

THROUGHOUT THEIR LONG HISTORY, the power of the Douglases attracted great hostility and envy, and many of their chiefs met with violent deaths. In 1440, for example, William, the 6th Earl, and his young brother were treacherously slain on the orders of Sir William Crichton, the Chancellor of ten-year-old James II. Crichton was concerned that the growing influence of the Douglases threatened the minority government of his young charge. So he invited the pair to a royal feast at Edinburgh Castle, which has subsequently become known by the grisly nickname of "the Black Dinner." For, while the Douglases were enjoying his hospitality, Crichton had them seized and put to death before the young king's eyes.

It would not be long before James II clashed again with a member of the clan. For in 1452, James II summoned the 8th Earl to Stirling Castle, in order to remonstrate with him about a treaty that he had signed with the Lord of the Isles. The Earl had been promised safe conduct but, when he refused to break off his alliance, James II lost his temper and stabbed the unfortunate man to death.

The doomed feast at Edinburgh Castle became known as "the Black Dinner"

Earlier members of the clan had enjoyed better relations with the king. Sir James Douglas (c.1286–1330) was a loyal companion of Robert the Bruce. Even so, he was capable of acts of great brutality. The most notorious of these concerned his home, Castle Douglas, which had been captured by the English. James labored hard to regain it – a struggle which formed the basis of Sir Walter Scott's novel, *Castle Dangerous*. At length he succeeded, trapping the enemy at church on Palm Sunday. Then he scattered provisions on the floor of the castle, piling the bodies of his prisoners on top of these, before setting light to the grisly heap. This gruesome act became known as "the Douglas Larder."

DRUMMOND

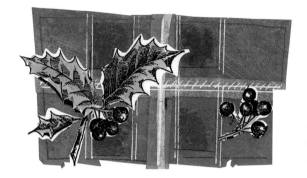

THE NAME DERIVES FROM Drymen (literally "high ground"), the territory in Stirlingshire where the family first settled. The founder of the clan was Malcolm Beg ("Little Malcolm"), who held the post of Seneschal of the Lennox in the early 13th century. One of his most notable descendants was Sir Malcolm de Drymen, who distinguished himself at the Battle of Bannockburn (1314). By strewing the field with caltrops (metal spikes), he crippled the English cavalry and helped Robert the Bruce to gain a famous victory. On a less auspicious note, Bonnie Prince Charlie is said to have worn a cloak bearing the Drummond tartan during the disastrous 1745 uprising.

DUNBAR

THIS IS A TERRITORIAL NAME deriving from the stronghold of Dunbar, which occupied an important strategic position close to the English border. Gospatric, the nephew of King Duncan I, was made Earl of Dunbar in 1072, and his descendants did much to frustrate the ambitions of their southern neighbors. The most famous of these was "Black Agnes," the wife of the 9th Earl, who successfully defended Dunbar Castle in 1337. Later worthies included Gavin Dunbar, who

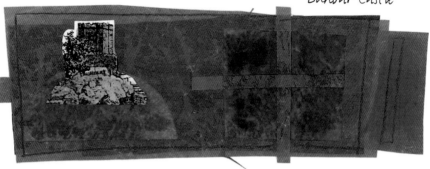

Dunbar Castle

served as Lord Chancellor in James V's reign, and William Dunbar (c.1465–c.1530), the poverty-stricken poet, whom Walter Scott described as "the darling of the Scottish Muses."

DUNCAN

THE ORIGINS OF *Donnchadh*, the Gaelic form of Duncan, stretch far back into Scotland's Celtic past. Dunchad (d.717) was an early abbot of Iona, and his namesake held a similar post in Dunkeld. There were

Dunchad (d. 717) was an early abbot of Iona

two Scottish kings named Duncan, both of whom met violent ends. Duncan I (d.1040), was deposed by Macbeth, as Shakespeare recorded in his celebrated play. Duncan II fared little better, and was slain by his in-laws in 1094. The Duncan clan was founded in the 14th century by Donnchadh Reamhar ("Duncan the Fat"), who fought in the victory at Bannockburn (1314). The Robertsons claim descent from the same ancestor and have always described themselves as the "Clann Donnchaidh."

Dundas

THE DUNDASES were an ancient family, who took their name from their lands in West Lothian. The charter for these estates is said to have been acquired by Helias, during the reign of Malcolm IV (1153–65), although Serle de Dundas was the first name to be properly documented, later in the century.

Erskine

THE CLAN takes its name from its traditional estates, the Barony of Erskine (literally "green rising ground") in Renfrewshire. The family developed close links with the Scottish royal family, when a daughter of Sir John de Erskine married the brother of Robert the Bruce.

The Erskine clan
were close to
the Stuart
royal family

Several clansmen reached high office in the 14th century, when Sir Robert de Erskine was appointed Great Chamberlain of Scotland and Constable of the royal castle of Stirling. Other signs of royal approval were soon apparent. The Erskines were chosen as guardians to both James IV and James V, as well as the infant Mary Queen of Scots. She rewarded her protector – John, the 6th Lord – by bestowing upon him the ancient earldom of Mar.

John Farquharson
of Inveraray was
a prominent
Jacobite rebel

FARQUHARSON

Farquhar is a Scottish variant of Fearchar ("the dear one"), a popular Gaelic forename. More specifically, the clan is descended from Farquhar, the fourth son of Alexander Ciar (Shaw) of Rothiemurchus, a family that belonged to the Clan Chattan Federation. The Farquharsons developed a more individual reputation in the 16th century, when Finlay Mor gained fame as the royal standard-bearer at the Battle of Pinkie (1547). This explains the family's Gaelic name, *Clann Fhionnlaidh*. Later generations of clansmen also became known for their military prowess. The most celebrated of these was John Farquharson of Inveraray, a prominent Jacobite rebel, who was popularly dubbed "the Black Colonel."

Fergus was a common name in the Celtic world

FERGUSON

Fᴇʀɢᴜs ᴡᴀs ᴀɴ extremely common name in the Celtic world, so it is hardly surprising that several different ancestors have been suggested for this ancient clan. The most distinguished contenders are Fergus mac Erc, the traditional founder of Dalriada, and a 12th-century Prince of Galloway, who built Dundrennan Abbey. In more concrete, historical terms, the oldest known branch of the family came from

Kilkerran in Ayrshire. They had acquired lands in this region by the 12th century and, in 1314, John, son of Fergus, witnessed a charter for Edward Bruce. The Fergusons of Dunfallandy also have a long pedigree. They hailed from Atholl, but were well established in Perthshire by the 16th century.

FORBES

THIS IS A TERRITORIAL NAME, which ultimately derives from the Gaelic word *forba* ("a field"). Historically, the ancestor of the clan was probably Duncan of Forbes, who held the family's traditional estates in Aberdeenshire, during the reign of Alexander III (1249–86).

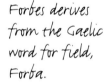

Forbes derives from the Gaelic word for field, Forba.

However, the clan also maintains a colorful legend, which argues that their ancestor was an ancient Celt called Ochonochar, who earned his position by slaying a giant bear that had killed nine maidens. This may be a folk memory of an early tribal ritual, since the animal was sacred to the Celts and there is evidence that a bear divinity was venerated in pre-Christian Scotland.

FORSYTH

THE ORIGIN OF THIS NAME is uncertain. The popular explanation is
that it comes from *Fearsithe*, the Gaelic word for a "man of peace," and
that it was initially applied to a churchman. Alternatively, it may well
derive from a place name. Robert de Fauside was a signatory of the
Ragman Rolls in 1296 and his son, Osbert, was granted land at
Sauchie in Stirlingshire (1306). He later fought alongside Robert the
Bruce at Bannockburn (1314). The person who did most to perpetuate
the glory of the family name, however, was the horticulturalist,
William Forsyth (1737–1804). His writings on the subject proved so
popular that the colorful *Forsythia* shrub was named after him.

FRASER

MOST AUTHORITIES RECKON that the Frasers came from France.
Various places in Normandy and Anjou have been suggested, most
notably Fresles and Freselière, and there is an ingenious theory that

The Frasers came from France

their name originated as a pun on a strawberry (*fraise* in French), featured in a Norman coat of arms. The earliest documentary reference is to Simon Fraser, who made an endowment to the Abbey of Kelso in 1160. In later years, the two main branches of the family were the Philorth and Lovat lines. The latter produced the most notorious of all the Frasers: Simon, the 11th Lord, who became known as the "Old Fox of the '45." After Culloden, he was captured and beheaded on Tower Hill, the last man in Britain to suffer this cruel fate.

GALBRAITH

THE NAME MEANS "foreign Briton," which suggests that the original Galbraiths may have migrated from the British kingdom of Strathclyde to a Celtic region. The name first appears in records which date from the 13th century, when Gillescop Galbrath was cited as a relative of the Earl of Lennox. In modern times, the most famous bearer of the clan's name is the noted Canadian economist, J.K. Galbraith.

The Gordon clan's popular nickname is "Cock of the North"

GORDON

THE CLAN TAKES ITS NAME from its ancestral estates in Berwickshire. These, in turn, were derived from *gor-dun*, which means "hill-fort." The family appears to have crossed from Normandy to Britain at the time of the Conquest, although the earliest documentary evidence dates only from the mid-12th century, when the name of Richard de Gordun appears in several charters. The fortunes of the family rose in the early 14th century, when Sir Adam de Gordun became Robert I's principal envoy. Their influence increased still further in the following centuries, as the Chiefs earned the titles of Earl of Huntly (1449) and Duke of Gordon (1684), although it is their popular nickname – "Cock of the North" – which provides the most telling indication of their power.

GRAHAM

THE FAMILY PROBABLY HAS Anglo-Norman roots, although some elements within the clan claim an ancient Caledonian warrior as their ancestor. According to this tradition, a chieftain called Gramus led an army of resistance against the Roman invaders, giving his name to a section of the Antonine Wall ("Graeme's Dyke"). In historical terms, the more likely source is an English manor called *Graegham* ("grey home"), which was listed in the Domesday Book. The owner of this property was a Norman baron, who belonged to David I's retinue in England and travelled north with him, following his accession to the Scottish throne in 1124.

The Grahams consolidated their position in their new homeland by marrying into the Celtic Strathearn family. This brought them the lands in Auchterarder, which were to become their principal estate. From an early point in their history, the clan distinguished themselves on the battlefield, gaining the nickname of "the Gallant Grahams." Sir Patrick Graham carried the royal banner during the war of independence, while Sir John de Graham was one of Wallace's closest companions, perishing valiantly at the Battle of Falkirk (1298). The chiefs were raised to the peerage in 1451, becoming Earls of Montrose in 1504. The 1st Earl fell at the Battle of Flodden in 1513.

It was in the 17th century, however, that the Grahams produced their most celebrated fighters. James Graham, 1st Marquis of Montrose (1612–50) was one of Charles I's most able generals during the Civil War, keeping the Royalist cause alive in the Highlands. His attempts to secure the throne for Charles II were less successful and he was executed in 1650, following a disastrous defeat at Carbisdale.

John Graham of Claverhouse, Viscount Dundee (1648–89) maintained the family tradition in his religious campaigns against the Covenanters. His greatest victory was at Killiecrankie (1689), although it also cost him his life.

THE LEGEND OF GRAHAM

THE MOST COLORFUL LEGENDS surrounding the Graham clan relate to John Graham of Claverhouse, Viscount Dundee (1648–89). He was educated at The University of St. Andrews and trained as a soldier in the Low Countries, where he served under William of Orange (the future William III). In 1677 he returned to Scotland, where he was promoted to Captain and instructed to snuff out the growing threat of the Conventicles. These were assemblies of religious dissenters, which had been outlawed by the Conventicle Act of 1664. In the 1680s, he carried out similar duties against the Covenanters (bands of militant religious reformers).

John Graham of Claverhouse was called "Bloody Clavers" by his enemies

In 1688, Graham had risen to second-in-command of the Scottish Army

Graham's skill as a soldier was matched by his ruthless determination. His enemies soon began to call him "Bloody Clavers," while some attributed his success to supernatural powers. Indeed, some propagandists for the Covenanters declared that he was a warlock, immune to any human weapon, apart from a silver bullet. This fearsome reputation, however, did nothing to damage Graham's career prospects. By 1688, he had risen to second-in-command of the Scottish army. As such, he led the resistance to William III's accession to the throne, even after his master, James VII, had fled to the Continent.

Graham's management of the Jacobite campaign was brief but glorious, ending with a notable victory at Killiecrankie (1689). On the eve of the battle, however, "Bonnie Dundee" is said to have witnessed a vision of a bloodstained Covenanter, walking ominously towards him. He took this as a signal of impending doom and indeed, on the following day, he was killed in the heat of battle. The immediate conflict was won but, without Graham's leadership, the Jacobite challenge in the north soon withered away. Even so, Killiecrankie did produce one further legend, for the site of the battlefield includes a wide chasm known as "the Soldier's Leap." This takes its name from Donald MacBean, a government sentry who was said to have executed the prodigious jump, as he fled in terror from Graham's forces.

GRANT

AMONG SOME MEMBERS of this clan a tradition lives on that they are distant descendants of Kenneth MacAlpin, the first Scottish king (843–59). Their name, however, suggests a Norman origin, as it comes from the French word for "great" *(grand)*. The family acquired land at Stratherrick in the mid-13th century and, in 1263, Laurence le Grand was cited as the Sheriff of Inverness. New territories were added during the reign of Robert the Bruce and, in 1493, the Grants inherited the Barony of Freuchie. Two centuries later, this was upgraded to a Regality – an unusual honor, which enabled the chiefs to rule like monarchs on their own land. Indeed, Ludovick Grant, 8th Laird of Freuchie, was popularly known as "the Highland king."

The name Grant is derived from the French word for great.

GUTHRIE

THE NAME MAY DERIVE FROM Guthrum, a Viking chieftain, or from Gothra, a forename. The lands of Gutherin are first mentioned in 1178, when they were presented to Arbroath Abbey, though they were purchased soon afterwards by a royal falconer named Guthrie.

The Hamilton clan takes its name from the town of Hambleton

HAMILTON

THE CLAN TAKES ITS NAME from Hambleton, a township in northern England. In 1294, Walter Fitz Gilbert of Hameldone was mentioned in a document about fishing rights. At this stage, Walter held lands in Renfrewshire, but his subsequent support for Robert the Bruce won him further estates in Lanarkshire. These included Cadzow, which has since been renamed as the town of Hamilton. The family's rise to prominence began in earnest in 1474, when James, 1st Lord Hamilton, married James III's sister. After this, they maintained close relations with the Crown, for which they were honored with a succession of titles. In particular, they were created Earls of Arran (1503), Earls of Abercorn (1603), and Dukes of Hamilton (1643).

HENDERSON

MEANING "HENRY'S SON," this popular name was current in many parts of Scotland, though the main branches of the clan can be found in Glencoe, Caithness and Fordell. The Hendersons of Glencoe cited Eanruig Mor (Gaelic for "Great Henry") as their ancestor. This shadowy figure was the son of Nechtan, a Pictish king. In Caithness,

Alexander Henderson (1583–1646) helped draft two important religious treaties

meanwhile, the Hendersons claimed descent from a son of George Gunn, a 15th-century chieftain who ruled with "barbaric pomp" at Clyth. The most distinguished of all the Hendersons, however, came from the Fordell branch. This was Alexander Henderson of Leuchars (1583–1646), who helped to draft two important religious treaties, the National Covenant (1638) and the Solemn League and Covenant (1643).

HUNTER

THE HUNTERS ORIGINATED from France where, according to tradition, they were official hunstmen to the Dukes of Normandy. They arrived in Scotland during the reign of David I (1124–53), and were granted the lands of Hunter's Toune (now Hunterston) in Ayrshire. The other main branches of the family were the Hunters of Kirkland and Polmood.

INNES

THE ORIGINS OF THIS CLAN are territorial. In 1160, Berowald the
Fleming was granted the the Barony of Innes by Malcolm IV. These
lands were situated between the rivers Spey and Lossie in Morayshire.

*John Innes was Bishop
of Moray (1407–14)*

Berowald's grandson, Walter, adopted Innes as his family name in
1226, when the royal charter was renewed, and the clan was officially
recognized by the Scottish Privy Council in 1579. Notable family
members include John, Bishop of Moray (1407–14), who rebuilt
Elgin Cathedral, after it had been burned to the ground by Robert II's
son, the so-called "Wolf of Badenoch", and Cosmo Innes
(1793–1874), the Sheriff of Moray, who worked tirelessly for the
preservation of Scotland's earliest historical documents.

IRVINE

ULTIMATELY, THIS NAME stems from Erewine, an Old English
forename, although by the Middle Ages, it also had strong territorial
links. In particular, it was associated with the parish of Irving in
Dumfriesshire. The clan is said to have Celtic origins, dating back to

William de Irwin, was the earliest family member of real distinction

Duncan (d.965), an abbot of Dunkeld, but this cannot be proved. The oldest records relate to Robert de Hirewine, who was mentioned in a charter of 1226, while the earliest family member of real distinction was William de Irwin, who supported Robert the Bruce and served as his armor-bearer. More recently, the clan's most notable figure was the American author, Washington Irving (1783–1859), who was descended from an Orkney family.

JARDINE

ORIGINALLY A NORMAN FAMILY, the Jardines took their name from the French word for "garden" *(jardin)*. Humphrey de Jardin was cited in a charter of 1178, while Patrick de Gardinus became chaplain to the Bishop of Glasgow a few years later. By the 14th century, the clan had settled in its traditional homeland at Applegirth in Dumfriesshire.

JOHNSTONE

THIS IS A TERRITORIAL NAME, which simply means "John's town" (in Scotland, a *toun* originally referred to a farmstead). It was taken up by several families, most notably the powerful Border clan, which settled in Annandale. Their first ancestor of note was Sir Gilbert de Johnstoun, who was cited in a number of 13th century documents. Adam Johnstone became Laird in *c.*1413 and was acclaimed for his valor at the Battle of Sark (1448), though the early history of the clan was dominated by a long-running feud with the Maxwells. This culminated in a victory at the Battle of Dryfe Sands (1593), and the subsequent murder of the Johnstone chief (1608).

*Johnstone,
a territorial
name, means
"John's town"*

KEITH

THE CLAN IS of Norman origin. The clan's ancestor, an adventurer named Hervey, was granted the lands of Keth in East Lothian, in c.1150. His son won even greater royal favor, becoming Great Marischal of Scotland in 1176. The Keiths were granted the title of Earl Marischal in 1458.

The Kennedys are the ancestral owners of Culzean Castle

KENNEDY

THIS POWERFUL CLAN has always been closely associated with the southwestern region of Scotland, claiming descent from Duncan, made 1st Earl of Carrick in the 12th century. In the 14th century, the Kennedys of Dunure became the principal branch of the clan, when John Kennedy acquired the lands of Cassillis, and their status rose still further in the following century, when his grandson married one of the daughters of Robert III. Gilbert, the child of this royal union, was created Lord Kennedy in 1457, and the family later went on to gain the earldom of Cassillis (1509). The Kennedys are the ancestral owners of Culzean Castle in Ayrshire, which Robert Adam transformed into one of the most beautiful houses in Scotland (1777–92).

KERR

THERE ARE MANY POSSIBLE SOURCES for this name, among them the Norse word *kjrr* ("marsh-dweller") and the Gaelic forename *Ciar* ("dark" or "dark-haired"). The two main branches of the clan – the Kerrs of Ferniehurst and the Kerrs of Cessford – can be traced back to two brothers, Ralph and John, who settled in Roxburgh in the early 14th century.

LENNOX

THIS IS A TERRITORIAL NAME, deriving from *levenach* ("smooth stream"). From an early stage, it became inextricably linked with an ancient Celtic title, for the Mormaers of Levenach or Levenax ruled over large tracts of Dunbartonshire, Stirlingshire and Renfrewshire. In the Middle Ages, this province was transmuted into the earldom of Lennox. Malcolm, the 5th Earl, supported Robert the Bruce and, by the end of the 15th century, the family was closely linked with the

Lord Darnley, husband of Mary Queen of Scots, was the Earl of Lennox

Stewarts. Lord Darnley, the ill-fated husband of Mary Queen of Scots, was both the Earl of Lennox and the son of the 4th Stewart Earl, while Esmé Stuart became Duke of Lennox in 1579.

The Leslies can trace their line back to the 12th century

LESLIE

STEMMING FROM THE NAME of their lands (*Lesslyn*) in Aberdeenshire, the Leslies can trace their line back to the 12th century. Their ancestor was Bartolph the Fleming, the son of a Hungarian nobleman. He won the favor of Malcolm III, who appointed him as the Governor of Edinburgh Castle and granted him considerable estates in northeastern Scotland. Sir Andrew de Lesly was one of the signatories of the Declaration of Arbroath (1320), which called for Scottish independence. In later years, the Leslies became renowned as professional soldiers. The most notable of these was Alexander Leslie (1580–1661), who served with Gustavus Adolphus in the Thirty Years' War, before returning to Scotland to lead the Covenanters. For his services, he was created Earl of Leven.

LINDSAY

THIS IS A TERRITORIAL NAME, meaning "the island of the lime tree." Sir Walter de Lindeseya was in the retinue of David I, prior to his accession, and his grandson acted as a hostage for William the Lion. Many of their descendants held high office, earning the titles of Baron of Luffness and Earl of Crawford (1398).

LIVINGSTONE

ACCORDING TO TRADITION, the clan takes its name from a Saxon lord called Leving, who settled in West Lothian during David I's reign and gave his name to the lands of Levingstoun. The family was also granted the Barony of Callendar, following Sir William Livingston's valiant action at the Battle of Durham (1346).

LOGAN

THIS CLAN HAS BOTH a Highland and a Lowland division. The northern branch traces its line back to Crotair MacGilligorm, a medieval cleric who founded a church at Kilmuir in Skye, and has always maintained close links with the MacLennans. The southern Logans, meanwhile, are descended from two knights, Robert and Walter, who helped to carry the Bruce's heart on crusade (1329). James Logan (d.1872) was a pioneering figure in the study of clans and tartans. In 1826, he toured Scotland, "with staff in hand and knapsack on his shoulders," gathering information about ancient tartans. His findings were published in *The Scottish Gael* (1831), one of the first books on the subject.

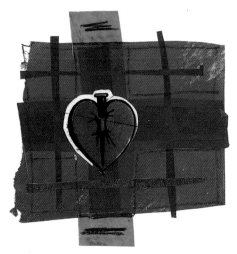

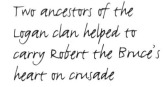

Two ancestors of the Logan clan helped to carry Robert the Bruce's heart on crusade

MacAlister

This clan name means "son of Alastair," the man in question being Alastair Mor (d.1299), the younger son of Donald, Lord of the Isles, and great-grandson of Somerled, King of the Isles. His descendants settled in Kintyre, where they became the hereditary Constables of Tarbert Castle, the most important stronghold in the region. Ironically, Alastair met his death through a feud with another relative of Somerled – Alastair MacDougall, the Lord of Lorne.

The main branch of the clan was later known as the MacAlisters of Loup

The main branch of the clan was later known as the MacAlisters of Loup, after the name of their principal estates (*Lub* is a Gaelic word for a river-bend). Godfrey MacAlister received these lands by right of a charter from the Earl of Argyll (1591). His descendent, Alexander, was a firm supporter of the Jacobite cause, participating in the battles of Killiecrankie (1689) and the Boyne (1690). In addition, the family had interests in Bute, Arran, and Stirlingshire. The MacAlisters of Glenbarr were also influential, and the modern clan center is at Glenbarr Abbey.

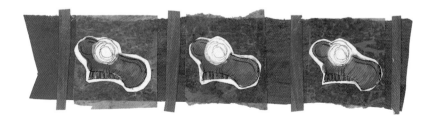

MacAlpine

Although MacAlpine is one of the smaller clans, it could hardly have a more distinguished pedigree. For the family claim descent from Kenneth MacAlpin, the ancient chieftain who succeeded in uniting the Scottish and Pictish crowns in 843, and who is traditionally regarded as the first king of Scotland. This in itself has created a certain amount of confusion, for a number of other, unconnected clans have sought to emphasize their links with this important figure and have thus adopted the title of *Siol Alpine* ("the Race of Alpin"). These include the MacGregors, the MacNabs, the MacDuffies, the Grants, the Macphies, the MacAulays, the MacKinnons and the MacQuarries.

The House of Alpin ruled the emerging Scottish nation, the much smaller highland nation than today's country, for almost two centuries, from Kenneth's accession until the death of Malcolm II (1034). It produced 15 kings, many of whom remain shadowy, quasi-mythical figures. The most notable, perhaps, was Malcolm II (ruled 1005–34), who won a striking victory over the Northumbrian people at Carham (c.1018). This enabled the Scots to seize Edinburgh and occupy the land between the Firth of Forth and the Tweed. Malcolm had no son, however, and on his death the crown passed to the House of Dunkeld.

In documentary terms, the family name can be traced back to the 13th century, when John MacAlpyne witnessed a charter for the Earl of Strathearn (c.1260). A few decades later, Monach MacAlpy was cited in similar documents; the image on his seal was recorded as a fox carrying a dead goose. The most famous family members were John MacAlpyn (d.1557), a religious reformer, and Robert McAlpine, the founder of a successful construction firm, who was knighted in 1918.

THE LEGEND OF MACALPINE

KENNETH MACALPIN occupies a unique place in the history of the Scottish nation. On the one hand, he is revered as the founding father of the nation, the figurehead who managed to unite the kingdoms of Dalriada and Pictland under a single crown. At the same time, he remains a shadowy character, shrouded in mystery and legend.

The most intriguing of these mysteries concerns the manner in which Kenneth came to the throne. He was not the first man to rule both kingdoms – Constantine, Oengus II and Eoganan had all managed it for a brief spell – but he alone succeeded in turning his rule into a permanent arrangement. Almost certainly, the secret behind his achievement was the rapid and total collapse of the Pictish hierarchy. This raised the suspicions of later chroniclers, many of whom declared that the union was accomplished by violent means. One source, for example, related how Kenneth invited the Pictish nobility to a banquet and then slew them when they were drunk. Another described how the assassinations took place at a joint council. MacAlpin's followers concealed their weapons beneath their robes and, after a pre-arranged signal, they set upon their foes. The details of these killings were probably invented, but there are strong hints that a coup did indeed take place. It is significant, for example that in 848, just five years after Kenneth's succession, the Scots transferred the bones of St. Columba from Iona to Dunkeld. The decision to move these, their holiest relics, into Pictish territory would surely not have been taken unless the future seemed very secure.

Kenneth MacAlpin
is linked to the
Stone of Destiny

On a more positive note, chroniclers emphasized the importance of
Kenneth's rule by linking him with the most potent symbol of Scottish
kingship – the Stone of Destiny. The earliest Scottish rulers were not
actually crowned; instead, they were inaugurated by being enthroned
on a sacred stone. This practice was very ancient, dating back to the
time when the Scots lived in Ireland. When they migrated to Argyll
and founded the kingdom of Dalriada (c.500), they brought their royal
stone with them. Its initial location is uncertain, although it was
probably installed at Dunstaffnage Castle or on Iona. There it
remained, until Kenneth MacAlpin transferred it to Scone, in the
heart of his new kingdom. This was intended to be its permanent
home, but Edward I, realizing its symbolic value, removed it and took
it to London. There it was placed beneath the Coronation Chair in
Westminster Abbey. It was only returned to Scotland in 1996.

The divine significance of the Stone of Destiny has inspired many
legends. Popular tradition suggests that it was the stone which Jacob
used as a pillow when he experienced a vision of angels ascending a

ladder to heaven. According to these sources, the stone was brought to
Scotland by a Celtic prince who had married the daughter of a
pharaoh. Many others told the tale of how St. Columba used the stone
as his pillow. As such, it was revered as a relic, after the saint died
while resting his head upon it. Yet another tradition relates that it was
the original *Lia Fáil*, the Irish "Stone of Destiny," which was taken to
Dalriada for the inauguration of Fergus mac Erc and never returned.

MacArthur

Meaning "Son of Arthur," this clan is traditionally based in
Argyll. Their ancestor was MacArtair, a supporter of Robert the Bruce,
who was rewarded with estates in Lorne and the keepership of
Dunstaffnage Castle. The clan fortunes declined after 1427, however,
when Iain MacArthur was executed on the orders of James I.

MACBETH

THIS COMES FROM THE GAELIC *Mac Beatha*, meaning "Son of Life." Beathan, later contracted to Bean, was a popular forename in the early Middle Ages. It had religious overtones, suggesting "the Chosen One" and was also associated with an 11th-century saint. Because of these linguistic variations, the Macbeths are often linked with the MacBeans and the MacBains. Other variants include Maelbeth, MacBehaig (the traditional spelling in Wester Ross), and MacVeigh, which was widely used in the Western Isles.

In most people's minds, of course, the name is principally associated with the Scottish king, who featured in Shakespeare's play. Macbeth was the son of Finlay, the Mormaer of Moray, and Donada, daughter of Malcolm II (1005–34). This gave him a legitimate claim to the crown, although he was still obliged to take it by force, defeating Duncan I at the Battle of Pitgaveny (1040). It seems likely that, for much of his reign, Macbeth shared his throne with Thorfinn, Earl of Orkney. Their joint rule was comparatively peaceful, enabling Macbeth to go on a pilgrimage to Rome in 1050. He remained in power until 1057, when he was killed at the Battle of Lumphanan.

Macbeth had no direct issue, although there were abortive attempts to place his stepson on the throne. Nevertheless, the Macbeths of Moray did become the principal branch of the clan, while the Beatons (also stemming from *Beatha*) were the secondary line. This part of the family was renowned for its medical skills. In Islay, the Beatons became hereditary physicians to the MacDonalds, while the Beatons of Mull performed a similar function for the MacLeans of Duart.

The Legend of Macbeth

The tragic villain of Shakespeare's *Macbeth* was based on a genuine, historical character. The real Macbeth was born in c.1005 and ruled from 1040 to 1057. He was a violent man, living in a violent time, but there is no evidence to suggest that he had any of the murderous qualities which the dramatist ascribed to him. In particular, it is clear that he did not reach the throne by assassinating King Duncan in his bed. Instead, he won it on the field of battle, after defeating his predecessor at the Battle of Pitgaveny, near Elgin. The real Duncan, incidentally, was considerably younger at the time than the old sage portrayed by Shakespeare.

Macbeth's personal claim to the throne was a strong one. His mother was a daughter of Malcolm II and his wife was the granddaughter of Kenneth III (997–1005). Moreover, with the Scottish practice of alternating the succession between the two main lines of the ruling family, it could be argued that Macbeth should have been king after Malcolm II. It may well be that the latter, in nominating his grandson (Duncan I) as his successor, was attempting to establish the southern custom of primogeniture. The conflict

between these two systems had created a number of succession crises since the 10th century, so there was nothing exceptional about Macbeth's actions.

Once he had gained the throne, Macbeth proved perfectly acceptable to his people. His reign was more peaceful than most others of the period. Indeed, the king felt secure enough to leave his kingdom for several months, in order to go on a pilgrimage to Rome. There, it is said, he made liberal donations to the poor. His generosity was echoed by that of his wife, Gruoch. She, too, has little in common with the Lady Macbeth of Shakespeare's play. One of the few facts known about her life is that she endowed a group of Culdees (an austere monastic sect). Gruoch married twice, her first husband being Gillacomgan, the Mormaer of Moray, a cousin of Macbeth's father. By this union, she had a son named Lulach, nicknamed "the Simple." After Macbeth's death, he was proclaimed king, but his reign was very brief (1057–8), as he was killed by Malcolm's forces at Essie.

Shakespeare's main source for his play was Holinshed's *Chronicle of Scottish History*. The gap of several centuries in reporting might account for some of the historical inaccuracies, but most of them were invented by the playwright himself, in a bid to please his patron James I (James VI of Scotland). The Stuarts, for example, claimed the legendary figure of Banquo as their ancestor, hence his detailed and sympathetic portrayal in the play. In addition, James had a particular interest in witchcraft and the nature of kingship – two subjects which featured prominently in *Macbeth*. James himself had written a tract on witchcraft (*Daemonologie*, 1597) and, throughout his life, was terrified that witches were trying to kill him. This fear probably stemmed from the famous case of the North Berwick witches who, in 1590, had tried to raise a storm against the ship which was carrying the king and his new bride back to Scotland. Similarly, the theme of regicide would have had particular resonance for Shakespearean audiences, given that the play was first staged in 1606, just a few months after Guy Fawkes' notorious attempt to assassinate the king in the Gunpowder Plot (1605).

Far from being an evil monster, Macbeth has great significance in Scottish history as the last of the old Celtic kings. He was the final ruler to base his power in the Highlands. Malcolm married an English queen (St. Margaret) and anglicized many elements of Scottish government. The remains of Macbeth, meanwhile, were apparently transferred to Iona, where he was laid to rest alongside the earliest Celtic rulers.

Macbeth is the last of the old Celtic kings

73

MacCallum

In common with the Malcolms, the name of this clan commemorates the influence of St. Columba (Callum is the Gaelic equivalent of his name). The family hailed from the Lorn region of Argyllshire, where they settled in the late 13th century. After 1414, the MacCallum Chiefs held the hereditary post of Constable of Craignish Castle.

The Macolls are associated with the area around Loch Fyne

MacColl

The MacColls are traditionally regarded as followers of either the Clan Donald or the Stewarts of Appin. They have long been associated with the area around Loch Fyne and, although details of their early history are scanty, they are known to have been involved in a bitter feud with the Macphersons.

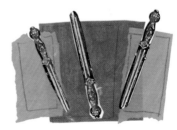

MACDONALD

The Macdonalds were the most powerful and prolific of all the clans

THE MACDONALDS WERE the most powerful and prolific of all the clans. There are no fewer than nine independent branches of the family and, in their heyday, they controlled most of western Scotland, along with outlying territories in Ireland and the Isle of Man.

According to legend, the clan traces its descent from an Irish prince, Colla Uais, who established a settlement in the Hebrides and ruled over northern Britain, prior to the arrival of the Scots. The oldest historical links, however, date back to Somerled (d.1164), the King of the Isles. Indeed, the clan derives its name from his grandson, Domhnall (Donald) of Islay, who battled against the Normans in Ireland and was even offered the Irish crown.

Donald's son, Angus Og, supported Robert the Bruce against the English and was rewarded with the islands of Mull, Jura and Tiree. The power of the MacDonalds was extended still further under his son, John of Islay. He gained possession of the remainder of the Hebrides, together with new territories on the mainland, and in 1354 he became the first ruler to bear the title of Lord of the Isles.

Through John's children, the clan began to separate into different branches. His first marriage, to Amy MacRury of Garmoran, produced Ranald, the founder of the MacDonalds of Clanranald, while a younger son from his second marriage became the ancestor of the MacDonalds of Islay and Kintyre. The other early branches of the clan were centered on Glencoe and Sleat. These different strands were eventually reunited in 1947 when, after many centuries, a new High Chief was appointed to preside over the entire dynasty. Its complex history is celebrated at the official Clan Donald Center, housed at Armadale Castle on the isle of Skye.

THE LEGEND OF MACDONALD

THE MOST FAMOUS of all the MacDonalds was not a hoary chieftain or a dashing warrior, but a courageous young woman who helped Bonnie Prince Charlie to escape from his English pursuers. The details of her actions were heavily romanticized in the 19th century, as chroniclers invented a love affair between the pair. Similarly, the celebrated Skye Boat Song was composed more than a hundred years after the event, and was deliberately created as a piece of Jacobite nostalgia. The real Flora MacDonald (1722–90) acted out of a sense of duty and loyalty to her clan, rather than from any emotional attachment.

She was born on the island of South Uist and given the Gaelic name of Fionnghal, which was usually translated as Flora. Her father died when she was just a year old and so, as was traditional, she was largely raised in the household of the chief of her clan, the MacDonalds of Clanranald. They were staunch Jacobites and enlisted Flora's aid in the aftermath of Culloden. As the militia closed in on the fugitive prince, she dressed him as her Irish maid and spirited him away to Skye. She also accompanied him on the long trek across the island itself, a perilous task, particularly as Charles made such an unconvincing woman ("a very odd, muckle, ill-shapen-up wife," as one witness described him).

After the escape, Flora was arrested and taken to London, but was released without trial as part of a general amnesty. Her later life proved no less dramatic. In 1774, she emigrated to North Carolina with her husband, only to become caught up in the American War of Independence. Her name was used to rally expatriate Highlanders to the British cause – the "Insurrection of the MacDonalds," as Americans called it – and she was forced to flee. She spent a bleak, lonely winter in Nova Scotia, before returning to live out her final years on the island of Skye. She had always intended to be buried in the sheet used by Bonnie Prince Charlie during his flight to freedom, but this item appears to have been left behind in Canada. According to local legend, it became the shroud of Janet MacDonald, one of her kinswomen in Nova Scotia.

Needless to say, there are many other legends associated with the MacDonalds. The most colourful of these concerns the ghostly piper of Duntrune. In 1615, the MacDonalds had designs on storming this Argyllshire castle. So they sent one of their kinsmen to check out the lie of the land, a young man who was noted for his skill on the pipes. Unfortunately for him, he was taken captive by the Campbells. Never slow to take revenge on their traditional enemies, they hacked off the piper's hands and buried him beneath the flagstones in the kitchen. Ever since then, there have been intermittent reports of the sound of ghostly bagpipes emanating from beneath the floor in this ill-fated spot. At last, in 1870, the kitchen was dug up and workmen discovered the remains of a skeleton. It was well preserved, apart from the bones of the hands, which were missing.

MacDonell

THIS IS AN ALTERNATIVE SPELLING of "MacDonald," which is specifically applied to two branches of the senior clan – the MacDonells of Glengarry and Keppoch. The former were descended from Ranald, the younger son of the 1st Lord of the Isles, and distinguished themselves on the battlefield. Alastair, 11th of Glengarry, carried the royal standard at Killiecrankie (1689), while General Sir James MacDonell performed valiantly at Waterloo (1815). Even so, many clansmen emigrated to Canada in the 19th century, founding Glengarry County in Ontario. The MacDonells of Keppoch, meanwhile, were descended from Alastair Carrach, the third son of John, Lord of the Isles.

The Macduff clan extends right back to King Dubh (967)

MacDuff

ACCORDING TO TRADITION, this clan has royal connections which extend right back to King Dubh or Duff, who was killed in 967. This line continued through Queen Gruoch (Shakespeare's Lady Macbeth), whose granddaughter married Aedh, one of Malcolm III's sons. More certainly, though, the first known chiefs of the clan were two brothers, Constantine and Gillemichael MacDuff, who lived in the early 12th century. At an early stage in their history, the MacDuffs gained the earldom of Fife, which entitled them to certain privileges. Among other things, they had the honor of enthroning new Scottish kings at their coronation, and the right of sanctuary at the MacDuff Cross at Abernethy.

MacEwen

THE EPONYMOUS ANCESTOR of this clan is said to be Ewen of Otter, who settled at Loch Fyne in the 13th century. His descendants held Kilfanan Castle and the Barony of Otter until 1432, when Sween MacEwen passed the estate to the Campbells. After this, the clan of MacEwen, their men broken, became clanless.

MacFarlane

THE NAME MEANS "Son of Parlan," a Gaelic forename which is usually anglicized as Bartholomew. The clan claims descent from a cadet branch of the Earls of Lennox, citing as their ancestor a man called Gilchrist, who held land at Arrochar in the late 12th century.

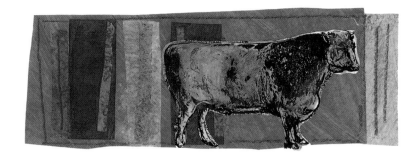

The MacFarlane clan has a reputation for cattle-rustling and feuding

His son, Malduin, lent assistance to Robert the Bruce, but it was his grandson, Parlan, who gave his name to the clan. Sir Iain MacFarlane, 11th Chief, fought at Flodden (1513) and Duncan, the 13th Chief, was present at the Battle of Pinkie (1547), though the reputation of the clan was later tarnished by persistent feuding and cattle-theft. Indeed, the full moon favored by these rustlers gained the nickname of "MacFarlane's Lantern".

MacGill

THE NAME IS THOUGHT TO DERIVE from the Gaelic *Mac an ghoill* ("Son of the Stranger"), although some have seen it as a contraction of *Mac Ghille Mhaoil* (a variant of "Macmillan"). The family appears to have been based in Galloway. It has also been associated with the MacDonald clan.

MacGregor

THE MacGREGORS CLAIM descent from the Scottish royal family. According to an old tradition, their ancestor was Griogar, one of the sons of Kenneth MacAlpin, who became the first king of Scotland in c.843. These illustrious origins are further emphasized in their official motto *Is rioghal mo dhream*, which means "royal is my race."

The family is first recorded at Glenorchy in Argyll, where they were granted land by Alexander II (1214–49). Their early chiefs included Hugh of Glenorchy and his kinsman, Malcolm the Lame, who earned his nickname fighting alongside Edward Bruce in Ireland. The gift of Glenorchy proved to be a tainted inheritance, however, for it lay between the Argyll and Breadalbane estates of the powerful Campbell clan, who did their utmost to dislodge them.

The MacGregors defended their lands robustly, meeting violence with violence. Ultimately, this strategy brought them into conflict with the government, which was trying to suppress lawless behavior in the Highlands. Accordingly, during the reign of James VI (1567–1625), the MacGregors were outlawed. Twelve of their leaders were hanged in Edinburgh, and the clan was barred from using the family name, from carrying arms or from assembling in groups of four or more.

This terrible situation lasted for almost two centuries, until the clan was eventually pardoned in 1775. During these dark years, the MacGregors were forced to live as outlaws or, in the words of Sir Walter Scott, as "children of the mist." After the repeal, General John Murray of Lantrick became the new chief. The clan's return to favor was emphasized even more firmly during George IV's visit to Scotland, when John's son was chosen to propose the toast to the "chief of chiefs."

THE LEGEND OF MACGREGOR

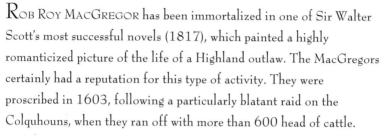

Rob Roy MacGregor has been immortalized in one of Sir Walter Scott's most successful novels (1817), which painted a highly romanticized picture of the life of a Highland outlaw. The MacGregors certainly had a reputation for this type of activity. They were proscribed in 1603, following a particularly blatant raid on the Colquhouns, when they ran off with more than 600 head of cattle.

Rob Roy (1671–1734) was a genuine, historical clansman, although perhaps not quite the Robin Hood figure portrayed by Scott. He operated as a legitimate cattle drover at his home in Balquhidder, although he also ran an early form of extortion or protection racket. Through this, he charged local farmers 5 percent of their annual rent, in return for a guarantee that their herds would not be stolen. This suggests that he had considerable influence over other cattleraiders in the district, although it also confirms that he preferred to steal from his two wealthy neighbors, the Earl of Breadalbane and the Marquis of Montrose.

Rob Roy was a contradictory figure. He supported the Jacobite cause and yet also joined the government forces at Sheriffmuir; he was jailed for a time in Newgate and was almost transported to Barbados, yet he was also a cultivated man, who subscribed to Bishop Keith's *History*. As time went on, his own escapades were overshadowed by those of his sons, James Mor and Robin Oig. They were tried and imprisoned in Edinburgh Castle for abducting a wealthy widow and attempting to steal her property. James managed to escape by exchanging clothes with a female visitor, but Robin was subsequently hanged for the offense.

MacIntyre

THIS CLAN NAME COMES FROM the *Gaelic Mac-an-T'saoir*, which means "Son of the Carpenter." According to legend, this was a reference to Macarill, a nephew of Somerled, the powerful King of Argyll, who was nicknamed "the carpenter," after boring holes in a boat in order to win his bride. His descendants settled by Loch Etive, where they became hereditary foresters to the Stewarts of Lorn.

Mackay may be linked with Aodh (d.1128)

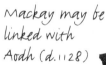

Mackay

THE SOURCE OF THIS NAME is *Mac Aoidh* ("son of Aodh"). The precise identity of the Mackays' ancestor remains a puzzle, although it has been suggested that there are links with the Aodh (d.1128), who was an older brother of Alexander I, and who became Abbot of Dunkeld. The first recorded chief was Angus Dubh, who married a sister of Donald, Lord of the Isles in *c*.1415. Angus's power was centered in Strathnaver, on the northwestern tip of Scotland, and this area became known as "Mackay country." His descendant, Sir Donald Mackay, was a distinguished soldier, raising the "Mackay's Regiment," which fought so valiantly in the Thirty Years' War. He was created Lord Reay in 1628.

Mackenzie means "Son of Kenneth", or "Son of the Bright One."

MACKENZIE

THIS CLAN HAS CELTIC ORIGINS, taking its name from *Mac Coinneach*, which means "Son of Kenneth" (or, more literally, "Son of the Bright One"). Its initial development is unclear, although the family did establish itself in Ross at an early stage. By 1267, the clan was ensconced at Eilean Donan, the famous castle on Loch Duich, and they soon gained a grant of land in Kintail. This was erected into a barony in 1508, and the clan chiefs were subsequently created Lords of Kintail (1609). The Mackenzies went on to make their mark in Canada. Sir Alexander Mackenzie (1764–1820) was a noted explorer, after whom the Mackenzie River was named, while another Alexander Mackenzie (1822–92) became one of the better known Prime Ministers of the Dominion.

MACKINLAY

This derives from *MacFhionnlaigh*, a Gaelic rendering of "Son of Finlay." The eponymous ancestor is said to be Finlay, the son of Buchanan of Drumkill. The Mackinlays were principally based in the Lennox district, although many of them migrated to Ireland during the 17th century.

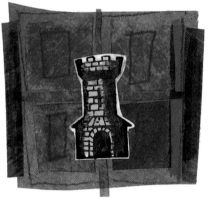

Mackintosh means "son of the Leader"

MACKINTOSH

This powerful clan takes its name from the Gaelic *Mac an Toisech*, which means "Son of the Leader." The term *toisech* could be applied to any of the ancient thanes and, as a result, the Mackintoshes were widely dispersed throughout Scotland. Nevertheless, the principal line is said to be descended from Shaw MacDuff, a younger son of the 3rd Earl of Fife. He was appointed Constable of Inverness Castle in 1163. The family gained added influence in 1291, when Angus, the 6th Chief, married the heiress to the Clan Chattan. After this, the Mackintoshes rapidly became the dominant force within this mighty confederation of clans.

MacLaren

THE ANCESTOR OF this Perthshire clan was Laurence or Lachrain, who was Abbot of Achtow in the 13th century. The family held land at Balquhidder, coming under the protection of the Celtic earls of Strathearn. As a result, their situation deteriorated after 1344, when the earldom was overthrown. The MacLarens supported the Jacobite cause, participating in both the 1715 and 1745 rebellions. Donald MacLaren was taken captive at Culloden, but made a dramatic escape while being conveyed to trial – a feat recounted in Scott's *Redgauntlet*.

There is a second, apparently unconnected branch of the clan in Argyll, who claim to trace their line back to Fergus mac Erc, the founder of the early Pictish kingdon of Dalriada.

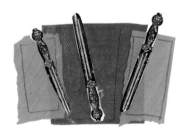

MacLeod

THE MACLEODS COME FROM an ancient Viking family. Their ancestor was Leod, a son of Olaf the Black (died c.1237), one of the last Norse rulers of the Isle of Man and the Northern Isles. His name is thought to stem from *ljotr*, which means "ugly." Leod held Lewis, Harris and part of Skye, which were later distributed between his sons. Tormod, the eldest boy, became the chief of the principal branch, the MacLeods of Skye (or the *Siol Tormod*), and inherited Dunvegan Castle, which remains their ancestral home. Torquil, a younger son, headed the other main line, the MacLeods of Lewis (or the *Siol Torquil*).

Malcolm MacLeod was granted lands in Glenelg by David II, but the most successful member of the Skye branch was its 8th chief, Alasdair Crotach ("the hump-backed") who secured a charter for the lands of Trotternish (1542), which had long been claimed by the MacDonalds of Sleat. More famously, he also commissioned the "Fairy Tower" at Dunvegan Castle and assembled a team of musicians, the MacCrimmon pipers. Their greatest hour was to come in the following century, when Patrick Mor MacCrimmon composed a famous pibroch for the 16th Chief ("Rory Mor's Lament").

In addition to their lands in Lewis, Torquil's descendants went on to acquire the Barony of Assynt in Sutherland (1343), together with estates in Waternish and Gairloch. In the 17th century, the chiefship of this branch passed to the MacLeods of Raasay. It was they who played host to Dr. Johnson and Boswell, during their tour of the Hebrides (1773). On this happy occasion, Johnson described the chief as "the perfect representation of a Highland gentleman" and praised his daughters for their well-bred manners.

THE LEGEND OF MACLEOD

Several clans possess some form of talisman, which is meant to protect the family in times of crisis. The most famous of these is the *Bratach Sith* or "Fairy Flag," which is owned by the MacLeods and kept at their ancestral seat – Dunvegan Castle on the island of Skye. According to legend, the flag will rescue the clan in times of great peril, if it is publicly unfurled. However, it can only perform this feat on three occasions. After this, an invisible fairy will arrive and carry off the precious object.

Clan historians believe that the flag's powers have twice been put to the test, both of these in battles against the MacDonalds of Clanranald. In one of these, the forces of the MacLeods appeared to swell to ten times their actual size, causing their enemies to flee in terror.

There are several different stories which relate how the object came by its curious name. The oldest account, published in Pennant's *A Tour in Scotland* (1772), stated simply that it was presented to the clan chief by Queen Titania. Another version suggests that it was given to one of the lairds by his fairy-wife. The couple had been married for twenty years, during which time the husband remained blissfully ignorant of his beloved's supernatural origins. These only came to light when she decided to return to fairyland, leaving him the flag as a parting gift.

The most colorful of all the accounts, however, concerned a 15th-century chiefain called Iain. When his wife produced an heir, a benevolent fairy came to Dunvegan, wrapped the infant in her shawl and sang him an enchanting lullaby. The child's nurse remained spellbound throughout this interlude but, when the fairy had departed, she found that she could remember every note of the strange melody. Ever since, this fairy lullaby has been chanted to all the MacLeod heirs. As for the shawl, it turned out to be the Fairy Flag.

Not all the stories about the flag's origins are concerned with fairies. One theory is that the object is actually the "Land-Ravager," the sacred flag which accompanied the Norse king, Harald Hardrada on his campaigns. Harald is said to have acquired the object when he was in Constantinople, and to have brought it with him on his invasion of Britain. The flag failed to work its magic, however, and Harald was defeated at the Battle of Stamford Bridge (1066). As his warriors fled back to their homeland, the trophy is said to have been left behind on one of their ships, when the flag was purloined by Godred Crovan, the ancestor of the MacLeods. The story may have some element of truth in it, for the MacLeods had strong links with the Norwegian kings. The oriental origins of the cloth also sound plausible for, when the flag was last examined, experts claimed that it was probably made in Rhodes.

The flag's powers are only supposed to be apparent when it is unfurled, though some believe that its mere presence may have some effect. In 1938, a serious fire broke out in Dunvegan Castle, threatening to reduce the entire building to ashes. As rescuers carried the flag past the blaze, taking it to safety, the flames suddenly died away.

MACLINTOCK

THIS NAME COMES FROM the Gaelic *Mac Ghill'Fhionndaig*, which means "Son of the Servant of Fintan." As such, it was probably intended as a tribute to Fintan Munnu (d.635), an Irish saint who preached in Iona. The family were based in the area around Luss, and were traditionally recognized as a sept of the MacDougalls.

MACMILLAN

THE NAME OF THIS CLAN has ecclesiastical roots: *Mac Mhaolain* is Gaelic for "Son of the Tonsured one." This indicates that the Macmillans were an old monastic family, belonging to the Celtic Church. The founder of the clan is usually cited as Gilchrist ("Servant of Christ"), one of the sons of Cormac, a 12th-century bishop of Dunkeld. During the Middle Ages, the clan gained considerable land in Knapdale, through marriage to a MacNeil heiress. Macmillan's Tower and Macmillan's Cross – both in Knapdale – still stand as memorials to their influence. In modern times, Kirkpatrick Macmillan (inventor of the bicycle) and Sir Harold Macmillan (British Prime Minister) have further enhanced the reputation of the clan name.

MacNab

THIS NAME STEMS FROM *Mac an Aba* ("Son of the Abbot"), a reference to the chiefs' role as the hereditary abbots of Glendochart. According to tradition, they won this honor, because their ancestor – Abaruadh, the "Red Abbot" – was a relative of Glendochart's founder. The MacNabs lost influence, following their opposition to Robert the Bruce, though their fortunes revived during the reign of David II.

MacNeil

THIS CLAN HAS strong Irish connections. It claims to trace its line right back to Niall of the Nine Hostages, the semi-mythical high king who is said to have ruled at Tara in the 4th century AD. One of his descendants was Aodh O'Neil who settled in Barra in *c.*1049 and

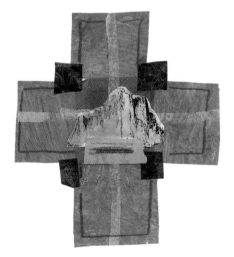

The MacNeil clan traces its line back to the 4th century

became the founder of the present clan. After this, the MacNeils rapidly established a power base in the Western Isles, with branches in South Uist, Barra, Colonsay, and Gigha. On the mainland, they were often feared as pirates. The most notorious of these was Ruari MacNeil of Barra, better known as "Rory the Tartar," who led frequent raids from his castle at Kisimul, until his nephews imprisoned him (1610).

MACPHERSON

ANOTHER OF SCOTLAND'S clerical families, this name means "Son of the Parson." As such, it can be found in many parts of Scotland, although the clan's traditional founder was Muireach Cattenach, who was parson of Kingussie, in Badenoch. Muireach was also a leader of the Clan Chattan, and the Macphersons played an important role within this confederation. Their influence has always been centered on the Badenoch region and it is here, at Newtonmore, that the clan museum is situated. This houses the Macphersons' most prized possession, its celebrated "Black Chanter." According to legend, this fell out of the heavens and was caught by their piper. When it is played on the battlefield, it always brings victory to the clan.

MACTAVISH

THIS CLAN NAME STEMS FROM *Mac Tamhais*, which means "Son of Tammas" (a Lowland form of Thomas). The family is generally regarded as dependents of the Campbells, although the MacTavishes of Stratherrick were closely linked with the Frasers. The Clan Tavish of Dunardarie was said to be descended from Tavis Corr, an illegitimate son of Gillespick. The charter granting them their ancestral lands dates back to the 14th century. The clan was active in the Jacobite rebellions, although they were compelled to fight under the banner of the Mackintoshes, since their own chief had been imprisoned by the Duke of Argyll.

MALCOLM

THE NAME HAS RELIGIOUS OVERTONES, stemming from the Gaelic *Maol Caluim*, which means "Servant of Columba." This refers to St. Columba (*c.*521–97), whose pioneering contribution to Scotland's conversion to Christianity ensured the popularity of the name. As a result, there were four medieval monarchs called Malcolm, most

There were four medieval monarchs named Malcolm

notably Malcolm Canmore (ruled 1058–93), who overthrew Macbeth and married St. Margaret. The name has similar roots to MacCallum (Callum being the Gaelic equivalent of Columba), and this has promoted close links between the two clans. Indeed, the MacCallums of Poltalloch changed their name to Malcolm in the 18th century.

MAR

MAR WAS ONE OF THE SEVEN ancient provinces of Scotland, which were originally governed by a mormaer ("great steward"), before the title was eventually superseded by that of earl. Rothri, 1st Earl of Mar,

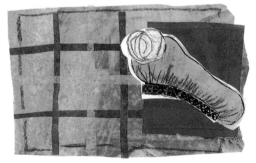

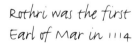

Rothri was the first Earl of Mar in 1114

was cited in a charter (1114) relating to the Abbey of Scone, while his successor, Morgund, was named in a document of 1152. The family were loyal supporters of Robert the Bruce, and this alliance was cemented when he married Isabella of Mar. Their grandson, Robert II, founded the House of Stewart. The earldom became the focus of a long-running dispute in 1435, when both the Erskines and the Crown claimed the title.

MATHESON

Matheson means 'son of the Bear'

THE CLAN PROBABLY TAKES ITS NAME from a Gaelic word for "son of the bear," although in the Lowlands it may simply refer to any "son of Matthew." The family was first mentioned at Lochalsh and Kintail in the west, where the Mathesons were granted land by the Earls of Ross. They may have been descended from the old royal house of Lorn. There was also a second branch of the clan at Shiness in Sutherland. These Mathesons acted as baillies for the Earls of Sutherland. From this line came James Matheson, who helped to found the famous trading house of Jardine, Matheson & Co.

MAXWELL

CONTROVERSY SURROUNDS the origin of this name. Some believe that it comes from a Norse chieftain called Maccus, who ruled over the Isle of Man and the Western Isles, while others maintain that it derives from Maccus's Wiel, a salmon pool on the River Tweed. The latter was named after a Saxon lord, who held land in the area during the reign of David I. Neither of these theories accord very well, however, with the documented history of the clan. This suggests that they arrived as Norman adventurers in the wake of the Conquest, and settled in the Borders. The first recorded chief is Sir John Maxwell (d.1241).

Sir Robert Menzies served as Prime Minister of Australia (1939–41)

MENZIES

OF NORMAN ORIGIN, the family came from Mesnières, near Rouen, and flourished in both England and Scotland. In the former, their family name became Manners, while north of the Border it took the form of

Meyneris. This spelling still affects the pronunciation of "Menzies," where the "z" is silent. Sir Robert de Meyneris made his mark at the court of Alexander II, gaining the post of Chamberlain (1249). Further estates in Glendochart and Glenorchy were acquired, as rewards for supporting Robert the Bruce, and the Menzies' lands were erected into a barony in 1510. More recently, members of the clan have distinguished themselves overseas. In particular, there are close links with Australia, where Sir Robert Menzies served as Prime Minister (1939–41).

MONCREIFFE

THE NAME COMES FROM the Gaelic *Monadh Craoibhe* ("Hill of the Sacred Bough"), which was bestowed on a Perthshire barony. This contained the stronghold of the ancient Pictish kings, from whom the Moncreiffes claimed descent. Sir Matthew de Muncrephe received a charter for these lands in 1248.

MOWAT

TRADITIONALLY LINKED with the Sutherland clan, the Norman Mowats settled in Scotland during the reign of David I (1124–53). The name is probably territorial, stemming from *Mont Hault* ("High Mountain"). Documentary references to Robert du Muheut and William de Monte Alto (the Latin form), date back to the 13th century.

Gilchrist Muir, Knighted for his part in the Battle of Largs (1263)

MUIR

THERE IS SOME DISPUTE about the source of this name. It may stem from the Gaelic word *mor*, meaning "great" or "big," which was often used as a personal epithet. More probably though, it signified that the bearer of the name lived on or near a moor. There are Muirs throughout Scotland, but the most prominent family were the Mures of Rowallan, who hailed from Ayrshire. Gilchrist Mure was knighted for his part in the crucial victory against the Norsemen at the Battle of Largs (1263). In the following century, Elizabeth Mure became the first wife of Robert II and the mother of Robert III.

MURRAY

THIS IS A TERRITORIAL NAME, deriving from the ancient Pictish province of Moray or *Moireabh*. The traditional ancestor of the clan was a Fleming named Freskin, although his precise links with the region are unclear. Some claim that he was a descendent of the Pictish Mormaers of Moray, though most agree that he was a foreign lord, brought in by David I to help subdue the area. Either way, Freskin's

heirs enhanced their status by marrying into the wealthy Bothwell family. This branch of the clan spawned the Murrays of Tullibardine, who went on to claim the chiefship in the 16th century. After this, their power increased rapidly, as they became Earls of Tullibardine (1606), Earls of Atholl (1629), and, finally, Dukes of Atholl (1703).

OGILVY

THE OGILVYS TOOK THEIR NAME from one of their estates, which in turn comes from an Old English term for "high plain" (*Ocel-fa*). The clan has Celtic roots, claiming descent from the Mormaers of Angus.

The Ogilvy clan descends from the Mormaers of Angus

Their founding father was Gillebride, Earl of Angus, who took part in an invasion attempt on England, before passing on his estates to his son, Gilbert, in the 1170s. The family became hereditary sheriffs of Angus, enhancing their position in 1425, when Sir Walter Ogilvy attained the post of Lord High Treasurer. At around the same time, the family acquired Cortachy and Airlie; the title was elevated to the earldom of Airlie in 1639.

Thomas Raeburn was cited as a vicar (1468)

RAEBURN

THIS IS A TERRITORIAL NAME, deriving from the lands of Ryburn in the Ayrshire parish of Dunlop. The first recorded mention of the name dates from 1331, when William of Raeburn witnessed a property deed. It became more popular in the following century, when Andrew de Raburn was listed as a burgess (1430), Thomas Raburn was cited as a vicar (1468), and Elizabeth Raburn was sued in a Lanarkshire court. The most celebrated bearer of the name was the portraitist, Sir Henry Raeburn (1756–1823), who is widely regarded as one of Scotland's finest painters. In keeping with the fashion of the time, many of his clients chose to wear Highland dress in their portraits.

RAMSAY

THIS NORMAN FAMILY TRACES its line back to Sir Symon de
Ramesie, who travelled north at the time of David I's accession
(1124). The clan's principal estates were at Dalhousie, in Midlothian,
and the chiefs later acquired the title of Earl (1633). Some family
members flourished overseas, most notably George, the 9th Earl, who
became Governor of Canada in 1819.

ROBERTSON

IT HAS BEEN SUGGESTED that the Robertsons are the oldest of all the
Scottish clans. Certainly, they come from very ancient stock, claiming
descent from the Celtic Mormaers of Atholl and the royal House of
Dunkeld. In common with the Duncans, they were also descended
from Donnachadh Reamhar ("Fat Duncan"), one of Robert the Bruce's
most able lieutenants. As a result of these connections, clansmen

*The Robertson clan is possibly
the oldest of all scottish clans*

initially styled themselves "de Atholia" or Duncanson. Their modern name comes from Robert Riach ("the Grizzled"), the 4th Chief, who brought the murderers of James I to justice. For this, he was rewarded with the Barony of Struan (1451).

The Ross clan takes its name from the Gaelic word for "headland"

Ross

THE CLAN TAKES ITS NAME from the northern province of Ross, which in turn stems from the Gaelic word for a "headland" (*ros*). The first chief was Fearchar, who bore the nickname *Mac·an t'sagairt* ("son of the priest"), because his family were the hereditary abbots of Applecross. Fearchar rose to prominence after lending assistance to Alexander II. According to one chronicle, he "mightily overthrew the king's enemies . . . cut off their heads and presented them as gifts to the new king." He was rewarded with a knighthood and, in 1234, was created Earl of Ross. The clan has several branches, most notably those of Shandwick, Pitcalnie and Balnagowan.

RUSSELL

THE FAMILY IS NORMAN in origin, although the source of the name
has been the subject of much dispute. It is possible that the name is
territorial, perhaps deriving from Rosel, near Caen, but it is more
likely to derive from *rous* ("red"), a common epithet for a red-haired
person. In *c*.1164, Walter Russell witnessed a charter relating to
Paisley Abbey, while Robert Russel of Berwickshire was one of the
signatories of the Ragman Rolls (1296). The name was popular on
both sides of the border. In 1333, an Anglo-Norman baron named
Rozel joined the English forces at the Battle of Halidon Hill, before
eventually deciding to settle in Aberdeenshire. The Russells are a
recognized sept of the Cumming clan.

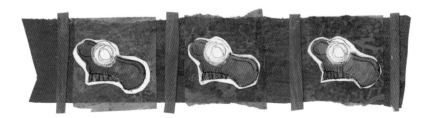

SCOTT

IN c.500 AD, a group of Irish tribesmen migrated from northern
Ireland to Argyllshire, where they founded the kingdom of Dalriada.
The Latin name for this Celtic people was the *Scotti* or *Scoti*. In due
course, they gave their name to Scotland, when the Scottish and
Pictish crowns merged, under the strong leadership of Kenneth
MacAlpin in c.843.

As a surname, Scott first became popular in the Border region,
where it denoted a Scotsman, just as Inglis indicated an Englishman.
The earliest documentary evidence dates back to the 12th century,
when Uchtredus filius Scoti (Uchtred, son of the Scot) witnessed the
foundation charter of Selkirk (c.1120). He had two sons, who are
generally regarded as the ancestors of the two main branches of the
clan – the Scotts of Buccleuch and Balweary.

The name of Buccleuch was first adopted by Sir Richard Scott, who
acquired the lands of Murthockstone through marriage, and the estates
of Rankiburn through his role as Ranger of Ettrick Forest. The 2nd
Laird of Buccleuch was a hero of the Battle of Halidon (1333), but it
was the 9th Laird who consolidated the family's position, when he
became Warden of Liddesdale and the Middle Marches in 1551.

During the 17th century, the Scotts of Buccleuch rose to even
greater heights, becoming in succession Lords (1606), Earls (1619),
and Dukes (1663). Their wealth and position was reflected in a
remarkable art collection, which can now be seen at the great houses of
Drumlanrig and Bowhill.

The most famous Scott of all, however, came from a secondary
branch of the clan. Sir Walter Scott (1771–1832) was descended

from the Scotts of Harden. He is mostly remembered today as one of Scotland's greatest poets, writers, and folklorists, although devotees of tartan also have good cause to remember him with affection. For Scott played a major part in making Highland dress fashionable once more when he organized George IV's visit to Scotland (1822).

The Latin name for a group of Irish tribesmen in 500 AD was Scotti

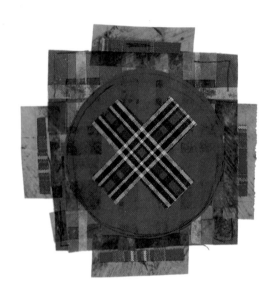

THE LEGEND OF SCOTT

THERE IS A CURIOUS LEGEND about the origin of the Scoti, which was first recounted in the Irish *Lebor Gabàla* ("Book of Invasions") and repeated much later in Hector Boece's *Chronicle of Scotland* (1526). According to this, they took their name from Scota, the daughter of a pharaoh, who married a warrior named Mil. Together, they travelled to Spain, where Mil died in battle, while Scota journeyed on to Ireland with her eight sons. Eventually, their descendants migrated to the west coast of Scotland, where they founded the kingdom of Dalriada.

Many legends also surround the figure of Michael Scot the Wizard
(c.1175–1235), even though he was a genuine, historical character.
In reality, he was a scholar, scientist, and philosopher, who translated
texts from Aristotle and wrote on such diverse topics as medicine,
meteorology, and astronomy. Like many scientists of the period,
however, he also dabbled in the study of alchemy and magic, and it was
these esoteric subjects which earned him the nickname of "wizard."
Dante included him among the damned who dwelt in his *Inferno*,
while Scottish folklorists concocted a wide selection of tall stories
about his magical powers.

It is said, for example, that Michael owned a magical horse, who
could fly faster than the wind. On one occasion they traveled to Paris,
where the beast stamped its hooves, causing every church-bell in the
city to ring; on another, he flew from the icy north to Rome, where the
pope was astonished to find that the beast was covered in snow.
According to the storytellers, Scott also had a team of demons, who
did his bidding. He set one of these to split the Eildon Hills, another to
dam the River Tweed, and a third to spin rope out of the sand, which
lay on its banks.

SINCLAIR

THIS CLAN TAKES ITS NAME from Saint-Clair-sur-Elle in
Normandy. A local magnate, Walderne de Sancto Claro,
accompanied William the Conqueror to Britain and his
descendants settled in Scotland. In 1162, Henry de St. Clair
received a grant of lands in Haddingtonshire and, in the following
century, Sir William Sinclair was given the Barony of Roslin
(1280). His son was present at the notable victory of Bannockburn
(1314), and was rewarded with property in Pentland. The most
powerful member of the clan was Henry Sinclair. He obtained the
earldom of Orkney through marriage (1379), annexed the Faroe
Islands (1391) and discovered Greenland. It has even been claimed
that he sailed on to America.

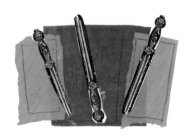

STEWART

No clan occupies a more important place in Scottish history than the Stewarts. From their earliest days, they held high office, close to the center of power, before rising to occupy the throne for more than 300 years. They were closely involved in some of the nation's proudest achievements, but also – in the careers of Mary, Queen of Scots and Bonnie Prince Charlie – in its most tragic interludes.

The clan takes its name from the office of High Steward, a hereditary post which the family gained in the 12th century. The first to enjoy this privilege was Walter Fitz Alan, who owed his advancement to the favor of David I (1124–53). Walter's family were Normans, who had long held a similar post (seneschal) in Brittany.

The Stewarts' rise to the throne was meteoric. In 1315, Walter, the 6th High Steward, married Marjory, the daughter of Robert the Bruce,

and their son went on to become Robert II (ruled 1371–90). After this, the family retained the crown continuously until James VII's deposition in 1688, apart from an 11-year hiatus, following the execution of Charles I in 1649. Both the Old Pretender ("James VIII") and Bonnie Prince Charlie ("Charles III") had claims to the throne, but these were never realized and they died as "kings over the water."

In addition to its royal line, the family also exercised considerable influence through its secondary branches. The most important of these were the Stewarts of Appin and Atholl. The Appin branch was descended from Sir John Stewart of Bonkyl (d.1298), whose father was the 4th High Steward, while the Stewarts of Atholl traced their line back to Alexander Stewart, the Wolf of Badenoch.

The alternative spelling of "Stuart" became popular in the 16th century, since it was easier for Scotland's French allies to pronounce. This was particularly important for Mary, Queen of Scots, who was briefly on the French throne (1559–60) with her husband François II.

THE LEGEND OF STEWART

No CHARACTER IN SCOTTISH HISTORY has attracted more romantic attention than the ill-fated Mary, Queen of Scots (1542–87). Famed for her dramatic love affairs, her devout Catholicism, her long imprisonment, and her execution at the hands of Elizabeth I, in death as in life, she was little more than a pawn exploited by different factions for a variety of political or religious purposes.

Mary was just six days old when she inherited the crown of Scotland, and within a year she was betrothed to the six-year-old son of Henry

VIII. Then, in 1558, Mary married the 14-year-old French Dauphin, with the proviso that, if she should die childless, her kingdom would become the property of France. But after just two years her husband died and she returned to Scotland. Elizabeth I was now the English monarch. Mary was heir to the English throne, and as a Catholic, she was both a champion of those who disputed the legality of Henry VIII's marriage to Elizabeth's mother, and a threat to Elizabeth.

In 1566, Mary married her cousin, Lord Darnley, although the couple were ill-matched. Mary entertained a series of favorites, most notably the dashing Italian David Rizzio and James Hepburn, Earl of Bothwell. The jealous Darnley had Rizzio murdered in front of his heavily pregnant wife, and this tide of violence continued when Bothwell had Darnley assassinated in 1567. Mary married Bothwell, but became implicated in the plot to kill Darnley. The Darnley scandal was too much for the Scottish people. Mary was deposed and in 1568 she fled to England, where she begged for Elizabeth's protection. Mary was found guilty of being involved in her husband's murder on the evidence of the "casket letters," which many historians now believe may have been forgeries. During her two decades in prison, Mary provoked numerous Catholic plots before Elizabeth finally agreed to her execution at Fotheringhay Castle in 1587.

SUTHERLAND

Although situated in the north of Scotland, *Sudrland* ("South Land") was one of the southernmost possessions of the Norsemen who gave it its name. The ancestor of the clan was Freskin, a Flemish soldier employed by the Normans, who also had close links with the Murrays. His great-grandson, William, was made Earl of Sutherland in *c.*1235.

Urquhart evolved from a place called Airchart

URQUHART

This name evolved from a place called Airchart, which may mean "a rowan wood." From an early stage, the family lived in Cromarty, where they held the hereditary post of sheriff. William de Urchard was the first clansman to hold this honor, though the most famous bearer of the name was Sir Thomas Urquhart (*c.*1611–60), the Cavalier author and soldier.

WALLACE

It is a curious irony that Scotland's greatest patriot did not come from native stock. The name evolved from *Waleis* or *Wallensis*, both of which were used to describe a "foreigner." These terms have left their mark on the English language, as the source for both "Wales" and "Welsh." Initially, however, the word was used more generally to describe anyone of old British stock. In Scotland, therefore, the name was usually applied to the Britons of Strathclyde.

The surname was in use by the 12th century, when Ricardus Wallensis was recorded as a landowner in northern Ayrshire (c.1160). His great-grandson was Sir Malcolm Wallace of Elderslie, so-called after his estates in Renfrewshire. Malcolm signalled his opposition to the English crown by refusing to sign the Ragman rolls (1296), and this spirit of rebellion was exemplified still further by the actions of his son, Sir William Wallace (c.1272–1305). This was the great Scottish patriot, who led his fellow countrymen to a famous victory at Stirling Bridge (1297) and assumed the role of Guardian of the Realm. In 1305, however, he was captured by the English and executed as a traitor. As a final indignity, his head was struck off and placed on a spike on London Bridge.

Inevitably, most attention is focused on the Wallaces of Elderslie, although there were also notable branches from Craigie and Cairnhill. The former was descended from Sir William's uncle, while the latter held land at Busbie and Clancaird (both in Ayrshire). Much later, William Wallace of Dysart (1768–1843) won acclaim as a distinguished mathematician.

THE LEGEND OF WALLACE

CONSIDERING HIS ENORMOUS FAME, relatively little is known about
the life of Sir William Wallace (c.1272–1305). Much of the
information we have today comes from Blind Harry, whose poem,
written c.1477, tells the tale of Wallace's exile and rebellion. The
poet claimed that he based his work on a contemporary account by
Wallace's chaplain, but most historians now believe that Blind Harry
added a number of popular tales and legends, which accumulated after
the patriot's death.

Wallace's life as a rebel began when he was a youth. He was fishing
at Irvine Water when five Englishmen arrived and demanded his catch.
William explained that the fish were for his crippled uncle and offered
them half, but the intruders became violent, and in the ensuing

struggle William killed three of his attackers. Now an outlaw, Wallace fled to the forests. According to local legend the fight took place beside an ancient hawthorn known as "the Bickering Bush."

At this time, the Scottish aristocracy were content to submit to Edward I of England. The outlaw Wallace joined forces with Andrew Moray and together they raised an army to oppose the English invaders and drive them from Scotland. The rebel army inflicted a humiliating defeat on the English troops at Stirling Bridge in 1297. The battle claimed the life of Moray, leaving Wallace, temporarily, as the unrivaled leader of the Scots. However, Wallace was not content, and he again engaged the English forces at Falkirk, where the Scots were heavily defeated.

Wallace continued to struggle quietly against the English until 1305, when he was betrayed to the English army and executed at Smithfield. He was hung, drawn and quartered, and his limbs displayed at Stirling, Berwick, Perth and Newcastle, while his head was placed as a warning on London Bridge. According to legend, in Newcastle Wallace's fingers seemed to turn and point to the north, directing his spirit back towards his homeland.

GUIDE TO PRONUNCIATION

AUCHINAMES *OCK-IN-AMES*

BALLINHARD *BAL-IN-ARD*
BREADALBANE *BREE-DAL-BANE*
BUCCLEUCH *BUK-LOO*

CARMYCHELL *CAR-MY-KEL*
CATTENNACH *KAT-EN-AK*
CIAR *KAIR*
COCKBURN *KO-BURN*
COLQUHOUN *KUL-HOON*
COMYNS *KUM-INS*
CROTAIR *KRUH-TAIR*

DONNCHADH *DUN-UH-KUH*
DRYFE *DRAIV*
DUBH *DUV*
DUNSTAFFENAGE *DUN-STAF-EN-EDGE*
DUNVEGAN *DUN-VAY-GUN*

EOGANAN *O-WUH-NUN*

FEARCHAR *FAR-KER*
FHIONNLAIDH *FIN-LAY*
FIONNGHAL *FIN-GEL*

GILLIES *GIL-IS*

LJOTR *LYO-TIR*
LUMPHANAN *LUM-FAN-AN*

MACBEHAIG *MAC BEG*
MAC COINNEACH *MAK-KYUN-AK*
MENZIES *MING-IS*
MUIREACH *MEW-RICK*

OCHONOCHAR *O-KON-ER*
OENGUS *AIN-GUS*

RUTHVEN *ROOTH-VEN*

URQUHART *URK-ET*

GLOSSARY OF FURTHER CLANS

ABERCROMBIE Named after an estate in Fife, the Abercrombies of Birkenbog settled in Banffshire.

AGNEW Probably of Norman origin, the Agnews were prominent in Galloway and held the hereditary post of Sheriff of Wigtown.

ALLISON Meaning "Son of Alice" or "Ellis," the clan is associated with the MacAlisters.

ANDERSON A Lowland clan, meaning "son of Andrew." In the Highlands, MacAndrew is the more popular version.

ARBUTHNOTT The name means "Mouth of the stream below the great house," deriving from the clan's estates in Kincardineshire.

BAILLIE Referring to the post of baillie (a type of magistrate), this name was adopted by several unconnected families.

BAIRD Originally from Lanarkshire, the Bairds also settled in Lothian and Aberdeenshire.

BOWIE The original clansmen were probably cattle farmers (a *boe* is a bullock).

BOYD A Norman family, who held the hereditary post of High Steward at Dol, in Brittany.

BUCHAN A territorial name, deriving from lands in Aberdeenshire. The Buchans were closely linked with the Cumming clan.

BURNETT From *Beornheard* ("Brave Warrior"), this family settled in Roxburghshire.

CHISHOLM Initially a Border clan, the Chisholms became Constables of Urquhart Castle, near Loch Ness.

CHRISTIE Probably a diminutive of "Christopher," the name was most commonly found in Fife and Stirlingshire.

CLARK An occupational name, which could refer to a clerk or a cleric. As such, it was popular in most parts of Scotland.

COCHRANE Said to be descended from a Viking chieftain, the Cochranes came from Renfrewshire.

CUMMING The family were extremely powerful in the early Middle Ages, holding three earldoms, but lost influence after opposing Robert the Bruce.

DYCE A Highland clan, drawing its name from lands in Aberdeenshire.

ELLIOT The principal line, the Elliots of Redheugh, were Captains of Hermitage Castle.

GILLIES An ecclesiastical name meaning "Follower" or "Servant," which probably referred to a monk.

GOW An occupational name, deriving from *Gobha*, a Gaelic term for a "blacksmith" or "armorer."

HAIG A famous military clan. Their ancestor was Petrus de Haga, a Norman warlord.

HANNAY An ancient Celtic clan, principally based in Galloway.

HAY Originally a Norman family, the name stems from the De la Haye peninsula in northern France.

INGLIS The name refers to an "Englishman" and, for this reason, was most common in the Border region.

LAMONT An ancient clan, which probably came from Ulster and settled in Argyll. They suffered cruelly at the hands of the Campbells.

LAUDER Originally a Norman family, the clan took its name from the Lauderdale district in Berwickshire.

LUMSDEN The clan takes its name from a place in Berwickshire. Branches of the family also settled in Fife and Aberdeenshire.

MACAULAY There are two main branches: the Macaulays of Lewis, who are descended from Olaf the Black, and the Macaulays of Ardincaple, in Dunbartonshire.

MACBAIN The family claim descent from Donald Bane, a Scottish king mentioned in Shakespeare's *Macbeth*.

MACDIARMID The MacDiarmids of Glenlyon – the oldest branch of the clan – are a sept of the Campbells.

MACFADYEN Meaning "Son of Paidin" (or "Little Pat"), the clan was first recorded at Lochbuie, in Argyllshire.

MacGillivray The name means "Son of Gillebride," perhaps referring to the father of Somerled, Lord of the Isles.

MacInnes An ancient Celtic clan, traditionally based at Morvern and Ardnamurchan, in Argyllshire.

MacKellar Meaning "Son of Hilary," the clan is a sept of the Campbells.

MacLachlan The clan's ancestor was Lachlan Mor, a 13th-century warlord, who lived on the shores of Loch Fyne.

MacLean Holders of the oldest recorded tartan. The name means "Son of Gillean," referring to Gillean of the Battleaxe, a 13th-century warrior. Modern clan members include the explorer Fitzroy MacLean.

MacNaughton Said to be descended from the Picts of Moray, the name means "Son of Nechtan."

MacNicol Probably of Norse origin, the family settled at Assynt, near Ullapool, and on Skye.

MacPhail Meaning "Son of Paul," the family has been linked with both the Mackays and the Camerons.

MacQueen Of Norse origin, this means "Son of Sweyn." The clan was first recorded in Argyllshire.

MacRae This is probably an ecclesiastical name, meaning "Son of Grace." The clan was renowned as a close supporter of the Mackenzies.

MACTAGGART The name means "Son of the Priest." The family was a dependent of the Ross clan.

MACWHIRTER This is an occupational name, meaning "Son of the Harper." The MacWhirters are a sept of the Buchanan clan.

MAITLAND Originally a Norman family, the Maitlands settled in Northumberland, before moving to Scotland in the 13th century.

MIDDLETON A territorial name, deriving from the "Middletown" of Conveth, in Kincardineshire (so-called to distinguish it from the *touns* or "farmsteads" on either side).

MOFFAT An ancient Border clan, said to be of Norse origin, and linked with the town of Moffat in Dumfriesshire.

MORRISON There are several unconnected branches of this clan, the most prominent of which held the hereditary post of brieve (judge) on the island of Lewis.

NAPIER An ancient Celtic family, descended from the Earls of Lennox. The name is said to mean "peerless" or "without equal" (*nae peer*).

NESBITT A Border clan, which takes its name from the Barony of Nesbit, in Berwickshire.

RANKIN The name is a pet form of Reginald or Randolph and, as such, popular in many parts of Scotland.

ROLLO The Norman family draws its name from the Viking chieftain who founded the Duchy of Normandy.

RUTHVEN This is a territorial name, deriving from an estate in Perthshire. The clan was descended from Norse settlers.

SEMPILL The Sempills held the hereditary post of Sheriff of Renfrew, before acquiring lands in Ayrshire from Robert the Bruce.

SETON Probably a territorial name ("sea-town"). Sir Christopher de Seton saved the life of Robert the Bruce and married his sister.

SHAW The Shaws belonged to the Clan Chattan confederation, sharing the same ancestor as the Mackintoshes.

SKENE By tradition, the clan takes its name from the *sgian dubh* (dagger), with which their ancestor rescued a king from a wolf.

STIRLING The clan takes its name from the town of Stirling, which has patriotic associations with William Wallace.

TAYLOR An occupational name (tailor), which was widely dispersed throughout Scotland.

WILSON Meaning "Son of William," the family is closely linked with the Gunn and Innes clans.